The Green

A Compilation of Plant Spirit Magick

edited by

Christopher Penczak

COPPER CAULDRON
PUBLISHING

Credits

Editing: Christopher Penczak, James St. Onge
Copyediting & Proofing: Mary Ellen Darcy
Cover Art: "Belladonna" by Nicole Lemire
Cover Design: Steve Kenson
Layout & Publishing: Steve Kenson

Notation & Disclaimer

Capitalization, gendering, and usage of terms by individual authors, denoting respect for certain entities, has been preserved, as has author usage of particular spellings (American vs. European).

Please note that none of the references in these articles are intended to offer medical advice, or to substitute for appropriate medical attention by a licensed healthcare provider. If you have a medical condition, seek the help of a licensed health care provider.

The publisher and authors do not advocate and are not responsible for the use of any medicinal information found in this book.

Do not take any herbal formulas if pregnant or nursing without first consulting your doctor.

Copper Cauldron Publishing does not endorse any suppliers or resources mentioned by contributors.

For more information visit:
www.templeofwitchcraft.org
www.coppercauldronpublishing.com

ISBN 978-0-9827743-5-9, First Printing

Printed in the U.S.A.

Starlight and Datura

By Gwelt Awenydd

Mother, do not worry that my bed is empty in the midnight hour.
I am out in the dark, healing my soul with Datura and starlight.
I am walking the silent, faery-haunted path that the moon makes on water.

Father, do not be vexed that your son is not the warrior you hoped for.
I have taken up swords of flame to turn back the armies of the ignorant.
I have fought angels and demons to be standing here today.

Sister, do not weep that I do not follow your king.
I am a servant of the Forest Lord.
I am a knight of the Holy Grail.

Brother, do not mock that I take not the bow to draw blood of bird and beast.
I have heard the call of the Hunter's horn.
I have wearied myself in pursuit of the milk white stag.

Family of flesh and spirit, take comfort that the Hidden Company surrounds me.
Rejoice, that I have seen the moon on the water.
Rejoice, that I have starlight and Datura.

Rose Pentacle by Laura Gyre

Table of Contents

Introduction

hen teaching plant magick and plant spirit classes, it never fails. Someone will always share a personal story with a particular plant, often one I've never worked with, or share an aspect of a familiar friend that I wasn't aware of, changing my whole relationship with the plant.

Just like people, plants have unique relationships with us. The side I might see can be radically different than the side you see. When we are working with people, we see a work persona, very different from the same person at home relaxing or out with old friends. Plants, while perhaps not invested in ego persona, do have different sides, and reveal them under different circumstances. Some are like business associates. Some are good friends, and some are even like lovers.

The Green Lovers speaks to that intimate relationship we can have with the plant world. Many who practice shamanic forms of plant spirit medicines can experience, and sometimes be perplexed by the loving and sexual nature of plant spirits. They are love for they are manifestations of the emerald heart of the earth, the verdant green that heals and empowers. They are lovers as so much of the plant world is about sex, the pollination scattering through the air, making us all intimate with their sexual lives, in every breath.

So when we were brainstorming ways to get students and community members involved in the Temple of Witchcraft fundraising efforts, and planned on a series of anthology compilations through Copper Cauldron, we thought the plant world would be an excellent topic.

With this book, we have many people sharing their secret loves with the greater community of plant magick enthusiasts. I've been blessed with so many great contributors sharing their love of their plants, ranging from well-established authors to current students just looking to share. With each one, I've learned something new and I'm sure you will too as you are embraced by these Green Lovers and open your heart to their magick.

Green Blessings,
Christopher Penczak

Part One:
The Balms

Agrimony

by **Raven Kaldera**

I first came to Agrimony through the Norse goddess Angrboda, first wife of Loki the Trickster, called the Hag (meaning Hagia, or wisewoman) of the Iron Wood, the sacred place of the Giants where werewolves roam. She is the Wolf Mother, the Mother of Monsters—warrior woman, sorceress, shapeshifter, grim and passionate—and She introduced me to Grandmother Agrimony, with whom She has a strong affinity. At the time, I was working with some rather nasty psychic stuff that needed regular clearing and purification and warding, and my usual herbs were hard pressed. "You need protection? Use this." Angrboda pointed the plant out to me in the seed catalog, and I ordered the seeds and grew Agrimony.

Grandmother Agrimony appears to me as a lean female warrior of middle age with close-cropped grey hair and a lined, weathered, narrow face. She moves like an athlete and is the sort that could be easily mistaken for male at first glance. Her gaze is penetrating and intense, and she counsels against impulsiveness. "Think about what you are asking for," she says. "Is it clear? How can a wight help if you don't really know what you want? Think through how this should go before you run out and cry for aid." When she is engaged as a protector, her work is swift, spare, and economical of movement; there are no flourishes to waste her energy, and she cleanses in a tight radius that nonetheless creates firm, tight boundaries of protection and a very clean area. She endows people with the will to change, to break out and make new changes in their lives. I learned, later, from another herbalist, that some Native Americans associate Agrimony with the Wolf, and remember Angrboda the Wolf Mother again.

Agrimony (*Agrimonia eupatoria*), also known as Church Steeples, Cocklebur, Garclive, Philanthropos, Sticklewort, Stickwort, and Egrimoyne, is a four-to-five-foot hardy perennial with toothed leaves, prickly burs, and tall yellow flower-spikes. As far as we can tell, she is long native to all parts of Europe and was widely known as a medicinal and magical plant. Agrimony has been one of the most praised herbs in the medieval herbal lexicon for its versatility in treating a wide variety of ills. The ancient Greeks drank Agrimony in a spring tonic for renewal. The dried plant has an apricot scent and can be added to sachets and potpourri, or made into a shampoo for thinning hair. The flowers were once added to mead. The entire plant yields a yellow dye when gathered in summer; fall-gathered plants produce a darker yellow.

As a common European weed, Agrimony has long been considered a strongly protective and purifying herb. As incense, she has a more intense and aggressive feel than Mugwort, and can be planted by doors for protection. This herb is a warrior plant, and can give "spine" to the weak, stiffening their resolve and helping them to leave bad situations. A sister to Cinquefoil and Tormentil (which like her are used as "repelling hand" herbs), she is said to work on hierarchical relations such as those in jobs or public interactions, clearing the way of obstacles and protecting one from the ill will of those in positions of power. Agrimony is a prime reverser of hexes and jinxes, throwing them back where they came from. Like Cinquefoil and Tormentil, carrying a leaf with you can turn away the malicious energies of others.

While Agrimony is not a narcotic in the medicinal sense—she is a mild muscle relaxant, but does not affect consciousness—Agrimony was used in magical charms to knock someone out by putting a sprig under their pillow. Numerous medieval charms recount this ability, claiming that the victim would not awaken until the sprig was removed. This may be a side effect of her ability to clear away an obstacle—*i.e.,* there needs to be some good reason why that person should sleep for a long time, so plan accordingly and check with Grandmother Agrimony before casting such a spell.

Shamanically, Agrimony is an important herb used in banishing unwanted spirits, including those that might be taking up residence in someone against much of their will. It can be drunk in tea or burned and the smoke blown at the person. Agrimony is also used in incense for a protective circle against unwanted astral intruders. Grandmother Agrimony steps forward with her sword and methodically makes short work of the unwanted visitors in a clean, silent, practical way.

To protect and ward an area—perhaps after it has already been recaned (the Northern Tradition term for smudging) with Mugwort or Juniper for cleansing—tie many twigs of Agrimony together and bind them with plant-fiber thread, let dry thoroughly, and then light the end of the Agrimony recaning stick and recan the area. Another possibility is to burn the herb as incense, but dry it thoroughly first; Agrimony does not like to be burned green. While burning, speak the following charm:

Agrimonia, Garclife,
Spear that cleaves the veil sealed,
Sticklewort and Cocklebur,
High Protector of the Field,
With the blessing of the Hag,
May all who would attack me yield.

A strong and cooling astringent, Agrimony is a good tonic for the gastrointestinal tract, to ease indigestion, mild intestinal bleeding, and colitis, and sometimes for gallbladder and liver problems, such as jaundice. The leaf infusion is a gentle remedy for diarrhea that is safe for children, and can be taken by nursing mothers to dose infants. Tea or tincture treats bronchitis (especially in drying up excess phlegm) and UTIs. Eyewash is good for conjunctivitis. Gargle is used for sore throats, and is good for nasal irrigation. May inhibit tuberculosis bacterium. Medieval war wounds were treated with a wash of Agrimony and vinegar. Poultice of leaves has been applied to soothe migraines. Don't take Agrimony if you're constipated, as it will make the problem worse. The acupuncture point associated with Agrimony – the door through which her spirit travels most easily – is Liver 2. Press on the point gently after taking her into your body.

A lesser-known property of Agrimony is that she is a painkiller of sorts, in that she helps tension throughout the body, but especially in the organs where constriction of the liver and kidneys can cause pain. Tense, uncomplaining, inwardly tortured people in general are helped by her, as are those with organ pain (gallstones, kidney stones, dysmenorrhea, bronchial inflammation, etc.). If the organ pain is bad enough that the client is holding their breath, this is an indication for Agrimony. In some cases it has had good effects for joint pain as well, if the original problem was organ-related.

One of Agrimony's medicinal actions that we discovered by sheer intuition is the ability, in tincture form, to relax spasming muscles. While she won't fix torn or sore muscles, when a muscle is actively in spasm, soak a cloth or paper towel in Agrimony tincture and press it onto the site for a while. We discovered this when my partner's deltoid went into a massive spasm from a yoga accident, and I had to use what I had on hand. I rushed into the pantry and asked the plant spirits to guide me, and Grandmother Agrimony spoke up. I only had tincture at the time – a big jar of homemade stuff – so I used it as what herbalists call a "fomentation" – a cloth soaked in medicinal fluid. It stopped the spasm in amazingly short order.

For a medicinal charm: When there is pain and overflowing of any organ (such as diarrhea), finely chop the aerial parts of

Agrimony and pour a pint of boiling water over a handful of the herb. While you do it, say or sing the following charm:

Garclife calm the cramp and flow,
May nourishment come fair and slow.

Then drink the infusion as a daily tonic to slowly convince your guts to digest thoroughly and avoid diarrhea, and to quiet the pain of angry organs.

What Grandmother Agrimony may do better than any other plant is to tone the internal musculature—the smooth-muscle pipes and tubes we can't consciously control, and that can become slack from various physical problems. In other words, she tightens everything up in places where we can't reach. That's a wonderful analogy to what she can do spiritually as a warrior-teacher as well. When you let her be your teacher (and you actually agree to work at it), she tones your courage and your will. She stresses the value of economical motion, of not doing more than is absolutely necessary to get the job done; no flamboyant energy-wasting moves, just practical precision. She detests sloppiness, and if you're willing to learn about the opposite of sloppiness, she might be willing to teach you a great deal.

Angelica: Guardian in the Garden

by Christine Tolf

y first encounter with the being Angelica was many years ago in my garden. I purchased a small potted Angelica and brought it home, and in my ignorance placed it in the earth in a truly unsuitable spot. Angelicas love rich, moist soil, a condition that did not exist in my sandy garden. With love and expectation I planted Angelica in the garden and visited daily, watered, and explained my need for co-creating a flower essence. As I have many times experienced, our green allies often grow beautifully under adverse conditions when there is an important purpose to the plant/person interaction. I was rewarded with a thriving plant that in its third year grew to human size and produced ample round umbels of flowers. Together, Angelica and I co-created a potent flower essence.

Anyone who meets Angelica will be struck with the plant's magnificent presence and will feel her protective, loving energy. This is a green genus whose use as a spiritual protector is consistent across cultures and throughout time. Angelica is believed to have originated in Syria, spreading to many cool European climates, where it has become naturalized. It is found growing throughout the British Isles and as far north as Lapland and Iceland. It prefers somewhat wet conditions, and can be observed growing around British churchyards.

Angelica archangelica has greenish white flowers that bloom from June to August. It is a spectacular looking plant, growing to an impressive height of five or six feet, or more. Angelica archangelica is a cultivated species here in America. Our native species is *Angelica atropurprurea,* or Masterwort. It has similar properties, but Angelica archangelica, the species that I grow in my garden, is considered the true medicinal. Wild Angelica can sometimes be confused with Water Hemlock which is a deadly poison, so please be certain of your identification. The Chinese Angelica or *Dong Quai,* a famous herbal ally for women, is *Angelica sinensis.* The genus *Angelica* is represented by more than 90 species distributed in temperate and sub-Arctic regions of the Northern Hemisphere.

Angelica

Angelica is considered a biennial, but experience has proven that this plant requires three years of growth to flower and produce seeds. The gardener who wishes to experience the fully mature Angelica every year will need to plant seeds or a first year plant from the nursery, for several consecutive seasons to establish a thriving colony. Angelica freely self-sows and produces abundant umbels of flowers and seeds on each plant. In bloom, the flower heads attract numerous pollinators adding to the dizzying hum of the summer garden. Angelica is a plant of the Sun, under the influence of Leo.

Angelica has been known throughout the ages as a protection against contagious disease, for purifying the blood, and for curing every conceivable malady from rheumatism to bronchitis. Mrs. Grieve, in her iconic *A Modern Herbal,* relates that in some parts of Germany, Angelica grows profusely in the wild. In that region, it is the local custom among the peasants to march into the town market squares carrying the Angelica flower stems, chanting an old charm, in a dialect now forgotten, even to the people reenacting this ancient rite. The chanted words and the tune are taught to the people in childhood, and may be derived from a Pagan early summer festival such as Walpurgis Night with which the plant may originally have been associated.

Native Americans rubbed the root of the native species, Angelica atropurpurea, on their hands to attract game with its permeating scent, attached a small piece to their fishing hooks for luck, and also carried it in their personal medicine bags for protection. Of course they also used Angelica's herbal medicine in brews for respiratory, digestive, and other health issues. The dried leaves of Angelica were also included in blends of smoking herbs or "kinnick kinnick".

After the spread of Christianity, Angelica became associated with the archangels and the festival of the Annunciation. According to legend, the Archangel Michael appeared to a medieval monk and proclaimed that wearing an Angelica root as an amulet would protect people from the plague. In the UK, Angelica blooms on the day of Michael the Archangel (May 8). This association led to the belief that Angelica was protective against evil spirits, witchcraft, spells, and enchantment. Angelica was called "The Root of the Holy Ghost." Yellow juice from the root is used as an ingredient of Carmelite Water. The root carried in a blue cloth bag is a protective amulet. Not only does it grant protection from negative energies, but its use also brings good or positive energy into one's life. An herbal bath prepared with Angelica will promote a healthy aura and provide a rejuvenation of positive energy to the psychic self.

Angelica is commercially harvested in Hungary, Germany, Siberia, and Belgium for the essential oil industry; 340 lbs. of Angelica seeds are needed to make one pound of Angelica seed essential oil. Essential oil is also extracted from the root, which tends to be stronger than that yielded by the seeds. Angelica essential oil has a woody, earthy aroma. In aromatherapy, the oil is used as a stimulant for the nervous system. In large amounts, it acts as a stimulant, but in small quantities, it is actually a sedative. Angelica is often used to treat mental exhaustion, nervous depression, and headaches. Angelica root oil is used as a flavoring for medicines and drinks, and the seed oil is used in perfumery.

The intense scent that emanates from a freshly cut stalk is never to be forgotten. Descriptive terms like "sharp", "herbaceous", and "peppery" do not come close to the uplifting, piercingly pleasant aroma that will pervade the room in which the hollow stalk or branch is placed.

To experience this plant of power most fully and understand her gifts, sit quietly in the presence of the freshly and reverently harvested stem. Place it on your altar and open your senses. Take a few drops of Angelica flower essence in a little water and slowly sip it down. The hollow stalk of Angelica is a

Angelica

plant signature that speaks of the shaman's journey. Enter into that green tunnel and deepen your meditation. You will connect with higher mysteries as never before.

Channeled information tells us that the Angelica plant was created by the Lemurians to soothe the effects of stress that they experienced while visiting Atlantis. Angelica is known as an herb of Atlantis and can be used to connect with Atlantean energies, visions, and mysteries. Angelica has also been used as a visionary herb to increase one's ability to see into other realities and times, both past and future.

The flower essence of Angelica infuses us with a feeling of protection and guidance from spiritual beings. It can be used for effortless acceptance of spirituality and a support for letting light into your life, as well as offering protection, strengthening trust, and reinforcing the action of the immune system during stressful times. It has also been used to get to the root of addictions. Angelica offers insight into the cause and nature of life problems and situations. Angelica promotes courage in those who are timid and fearful and helps us face the unknown by strengthening our connection to the Angelic realm. It is said to bring a deeper understanding of inner light, insight and inspiration in one's life purpose and puts us in touch with that part of the inner self that is immortal.

For use in medicine and magic, the root is collected in the autumn of its first or second year, before it produces flowers. If it is very thick it can be cut lengthwise to hasten drying. Some magickal spells require use of the whole root, so understand your needs and take this into account when harvesting. The leaves are collected in June, before the plant flowers. The stems are often candied and used as an after dinner treat to aid digestion. Seeds and foliage are used in some preparations, but the root is considered the "official" or primary source of herbal medicine. Herbally, Angelica improves circulation and warms the body. It can be a useful ingredient in blends for coughs and colds. Angelica is well known as a carminative (an herb which relieves gas and griping bowel pains). I like to include it in a formula for digestive bitters.

Practitioners of Hoodoo folk magic, or root work, use Angelica root in many workings involving protection. It is an important ingredient of the famous "Fiery Wall of Protection" spell. I have used this spell myself and found it to be very powerful. Using my own freshly harvested and heavily fragrant root of Angelica gave this work an extra boost of power.

Whenever you personalize your magick through the use of herbs which were grown and harvested with respect, the intensity of the work deepens. However, not everyone can grow their own magickal herb supply. If you are unable to speak to the growing plant and have interaction with it, I always advise students to interact with the jars of herbs in the apothecary. Herbs enjoy praise and can react to direction from the practitioner. Explain the purpose of your working to the herbs and ask respectfully for their aid. Plant spirit is present in harvested dried herb, essential oils, infused oils, hydrosols, and other herbal products.

Sources

http://zipcodezoo.com/Key/Plantae/Angelica_Genus.asp (accessed February 19, 2011)

Mrs. M. Grieve, *A Modern Herbal,* vol. I (New York: Dover Publications, Inc, 1982), 37.

Daniel E Moerman, *Native American Medicinal Plants,* (Portland: Timber Press, Inc., 2009), 67.

Smoking and Pipes, *http://www.cowasuck.org/lifestyle/pipes.cfm* (accessed February 19, 2011)

http://www.anandaapothecary.com/aromatherapy-essential-oils/angelica-essential-oil.html (accessed February 19, 2011)

Borage

By Stevie Grant

orage (*Borago officinalis*) has found a special place in my heart, ever since I introduced it to my sprawling herb garden at Ostara several years ago. I planted it as a start from a local nursery without knowing much about it other than that it had been in their herb section and that it liked full sun. The start had perky fuzzy leaves. It grew to about three feet high by Midsummer, its central stalk thick but fuzzy like its leaves. The botanically simple leaves, five inches long at the bottom of the plant, became smaller and smaller toward the top. Each blue flower, almost the shade of periwinkle, had five pointed petals sitting on a bed of five petaled leaflike structures (sepals) that had enclosed the bud. In the center of the ring of petals and sepals was a tiny white ring around a yellow ring from which emerged the green stamens and pistil. These small flowers clustered along its branches, making the entire plant look dramatic against the darker greens of other herbs. Halfway between Midsummer and Lammas, the plant flopped over. I tried to stake it upright, but it twisted and curled around itself, so I just let it be.

Sketch of borage flower, also known as star flower

A couple of weeks before Samhain that first year, I went outside to do the Plant Spirit Communication exercise in Christopher Penczak's The Temple of Shamanic Witchcraft, my first experience with the spirit of a specific plant. The Borage was near the edge of the herb garden, bordering the grass. Amid brown foliage, it still had a lot of greenery and a single late bloom. I sat cross-legged in front of it and set nearby a watering can of water. The day was dry, sunny, and quite windy. I put the hood of my coat up over my head, closed my eyes, went into a meditative state, asked Goddess and God for guidance, and breathed in energy from Earth and Sky.

In my inner mind, I said I wished to communicate and connect with the Borage plant. I heard "Touch me." Eyes still closed, I physically reached out to touch the fuzzy, almost prickly leaves. I asked for the plant spirit ally. I waited but saw nothing except the brightness from the sun, yet I sensed my aura and that of the Borage overlapping, our energies mingling. I felt myself gently rubbing whatever I was holding physically of the plant. I asked it to tell me about its spirit medicine, powers, and mysteries. Borage Spirit communicated in words, almost like the voice of a sprite, high and tingly. He said he was for courage and also for better sight.

"You can make a poultice for anywhere on your body," Borage Spirit said. "Make a tincture."

"I guess that means you're willing to partner with me," I said.

"Yes."

"What parts do I use?"

"My leaves. And my stems, flowers, and roots, too."

"And you aren't poisonous?"

"Not too much." Borage Spirit laughed.

"So you have a sense of humor."

"Yes, yes, it's part of courage."

I saw with my inner eyes that we were cocooned in an area of no wind. I sensed the calmness of courage. I seemed to be inside the plant, as if surrounded by its tangle of leaves and branches. The sun beamed into the cocoon.

Borage Spirit thanked me for getting rid of the soapwort I'd planted next to him a couple of months before. "Not that there's anything wrong with that plant," Borage Spirit said, "but I'm basically wild and tend to pop up here and there, and I need room to do that." He told me he felt fine growing in my garden, that I could even cultivate him by shaping where he grows, pulling up starts, transplanting others, and cutting him back. I asked if he'd come back next year, and he said yes, from his seeds, not from the old plant. I asked when I should tincture him. "Anytime", he said; "You don't have to do it right away." Borage Spirit added that having a few drops of the tincture 2 days out of 7 would be beneficial. He pointed out that he's very hardy, even though he bends in peculiar ways if I try to stake him, and may even seem to break in places, but his essence stays intact. He told me to remember this with regard to courage.

Borage Spirit said his fuzzy little stickers wouldn't hurt me, and told me to smell him. I did physically, my eyes still closed, inhaling whiffs that resembled fresh cucumber. Then we sat together in the sunny stillness of our little bubble. I knew it was windy all around because I could physically hear the wind chimes from the sun porch. The sunlight in our bubble was still quite bright. Borage Spirit then said that was enough for now so that I'd remember everything. I thanked him and blew on him. He blew back oxygen to me. We exchanged oxygen and carbon dioxide back and forth several times. When we stopped, I saw Borage Spirit. He came from or was part of the center of the plant, the curled branches and leaves were his hair, maybe even his body. He seemed to sing along with the wind chimes, his song like a gentle breath of air. I smiled with joyful teary eyes.

I thanked Borage Spirit, the Goddess and God, and returned to normal waking consciousness. I opened my eyes, gave myself clearance and balance, and grounded. The immediate area around me, for a diameter of several feet or so, was still calm, the wind blowing beyond. The sun, as I'd seen inwardly, was streaming more intensely into this bubble than onto the surrounding area. I felt a sense of awe. I thanked the plant again, and then watered it from the watering can.

I was moved by the experience and amazed that I was able to corroborate in my reading what I learned from Borage Spirit. The following year I found no offspring of the original Borage plant until almost Lammas. The new Borage had been growing under the thick leaves of another plant and was hidden from view until it grew big enough to peek out beyond this foliage. I was so happy to see it! I asked if I could harvest a small portion. When I got a yes, I carefully cut a branch and blew on the rest of the plant to thank him. I put up a tincture, which was ready by Mabon. It helped support me during the intense preparation for my shadow ritual at the end of *The Temple of Shamanic Witchcraft* at Samhain. Since then, I've continued to partner with Borage in a variety of ways.

Borage Spirit may have been coy when he said he was only mildly toxic, but he added sound advice by telling me I could ingest a few drops of his tincture two out of every seven days. Borage leaves contain small amounts of Amabiline, an alkaloid that in large quantities is liver-toxic. Researchers at Sloan-Kettering suggest no more than 1 mcg per day and, if possible, to use oils free from these alkaloids. But I don't buy commercial Borage oil; I grow and harvest the plant myself. When using a tincture from the whole plant, I measure out 2-3 drops at a time. For sustained use, I make a flower essence, a dilute solution of the tincture. I could also make a tincture, oil, or tea from just the flowers or the seeds, since the toxin is in the leaves and stems.

Borage, at Midsummer, center foreground. It is surrounded by Heuchera flowers, Lupins, Golden Calendula, dark leaves of Black-eyed Susans (not in bloom), and tall stalks of Oregano. Photo courtesy of Mark Borgmier.

Borage, whose gender is masculine, is ruled by the planet Jupiter and the astrological sign of Leo, which is ruled by the Sun. Borage is listed in most magickal books as an herb of courage and bravery, but it can also be used for inner strength of character, joy, purification, protection, and psychic vision (the "better sight" that Borage Spirit told me about in the meditation). I've ingested a few drops of Borage tincture or flower essence just before or during a meditation or ritual. Borage is also beneficial in amulets, potions, baths, and washes. The dried and powdered roots make good incense.

During one shamanic journey, Borage Spirit had me shapeshift into a Borage plant. A deep, large taproot started at my tailbone and went into the ground. My body became the leaves and flowers. It was sunny around me, more so than elsewhere. I was either emanating radiance or attracting the sunshine, or both. I felt tendrils growing out of me from various places. At first I was straight as I rose up from the Earth. Then I became heavy and bent over, my branches thick and pliable. I felt bees on me, sucking nectar. They fed me bits of carbon dioxide and breathed in my oxygen. I felt butterflies land on my flowers, their white wings fluttering. A slug sloshed its way underneath my branches but did not stay because of my prickly leaves and stems. Borage Spirit said, "We like tomatoes and help them if they're nearby." He added, "I'm protective because of my sunny disposition. I don't fight and I don't withdraw from conflict. Instead, I radiate so much sunshine and goodwill that conflict disperses or disappears because there's no room for it."

My consciousness went into my deep root. In the dark under the Earth, I felt little rootlets reaching out to soak up nutrients. Solidly grounded in the Earth, I was at home with myself, my safety and sense of belonging coming from within, even as I was connected to everything else and interacted with what was around me. My strength was gentle but firm. My consciousness then rose into the flowers and many seeds. I knew my seeds would fall nearby or be carried by the wind so that my offspring could grow unexpectedly in many places, spreading their joy, courage, and sunny disposition.

After I returned to my human body, I saw Borage's five-pointed blue flowers with the circle in the center. As I stared at the circle of one flower, the petals twirled around and around. Borage Spirit said, "the spirit is in the center. The spiritual center." Pentagram-shaped Borage can act as a gateway, not only opening out to the physical world but also aiding communication with the Divine.

Medicinally, Borage helps reduce inflammation in rheumatoid arthritis, may regulate metabolism and the hormonal system, may alleviate menopausal discomforts such as hot flashes, and has been used in cases of chest congestion and cough. A poultice of Borage can be applied topically to diminish some forms of eczema and dermatitis. As an eyewash, Borage tea soothes tired or irritated eyes. After experiencing Borage's humor and sunny disposition, I was not surprised to find that it has also been used as an antidepressant. I reach for it to boost my courage in difficult situations.

Many cultures have used Borage as a culinary herb or vegetable. The younger leaves, eaten fresh in salad, taste just as I smelled them, like mild cucumber. I had to get used to the fuzzy texture, which can be reduced by sautéing. I found a number of recipes online, but, because of the toxicity, however mild, I'm careful not to prepare a whole mass of the leaves, fresh or cooked, too often. As a food, I consider Borage leaves a delicacy, to use only occasionally and sparingly and never if one is pregnant. The safer flowers taste sweet, like honey. Also great in salad, they add their unusual blue to the other more typical vegetable colors. They can be candied as a garnish for cakes. Borage makes a beautiful bouquet on the table.

In the garden, Borage flowers attract bees and butterflies, no doubt responsible for calling it Bee Bread or Bee Plant. Borage is a good companion plant, said to protect legumes, spinach, brassicas, strawberries, and tomatoes from their typical pests. Unless Borage seeds are planted in a desired location, though, new starts will appear wherever the wind, squirrels, or birds deposit the seeds of last year's plant. It's relatively easy to transplant young starts but gets more difficult with more mature Borage because of the deep taproot. Borage is a good drought-tolerant ground cover and soil binder.

While writing this article, I journeyed again to the Spirit of Borage, who gave me a message for you, the readers. He said, "Tell them to use me for courage and bravery. Not to fight, though. I am masculine in strength, but not the brute strength of the warrior or of the stereotypical male. I am the strength that perseveres. And I protect by surrounding one with sunshine, even humor, laughter, smiles."

Sources

Alchemy Works. "Borago officinalis Borage." Retrieved from *http://www.alchemy-works.com/borago_officinalis.html* on February 11, 2011.

Beyerl, Paul. *The Master Book of Herbalism.* Custer WA: Phoenix Publishing, 1984.

Beyerl, Paul. *A Compendium of Herbal Magick.* Custer WA: Phoenix Publishing, 1998.

Brenzel, Kathleen Norris (ed.). *Sunset Western Garden Book,* 8th edit. Menlo Park CA: Sunset Publishing, 2007.

Crawford, Amanda McQuade. *The Herbal Menopause Book.* Freedom CA: The Crossing Press, 1996.

Cunningham, Scott. *Encyclopedia of Magical Herbs.* Woodbury MN: Llewellyn, 1985.

Greer, John Michael. *Natural Magic: Potions and Powers from the Magical Garden.* St. Paul MN: Llewellyn, 2000.

Nichols Garden Nursery Catalog. Albany OR: Nichols Garden Nursery, 2011.

Penczak, Christopher. *The Temple of Shamanic Witchcraft.* St. Paul MN: Llewellyn, 2005.

Ritchason, Jack. *The Little Herb Encyclopedia,* 3rd edit. Pleasant Grove UT: Woodland Health Books, 1995.

Robertson, Laurel, Carol Flinders, and Brian Ruppenthal. *The New Laurel's Kitchen.* Berkeley CA: Ten Speed Press, 1986.

Sloan-Kettering. "Borage." Retrieved from *http://www.mskcc.org/mskcc/html/69148.cfm* on February 23, 2011.

Weed, Susun S. *New Menopausal Years: The Wise Woman Way.* Woodstock NY: Ash Tree Publishing, 2002.

Wikipedia, the free encyclopedia. "Borage." Retrieved from *http://en.wikipedia.org/wiki/Borage* on February 23, 2011.

Sweet Basil

By Silvermoone

he scent of Basil's sweetness is palpable, whether in dry or fresh form, its fragrance has always opened up the channels of love for me. Though the essence of love is just one of the properties Sweet Basil has to offer, it is all tied together in the energies of love, invoking the deepest purity of Self.

While there are a few variations of Basil, Sweet Basil's energies range from fertility, to love, to purification, and even to death. A wide range of qualities, it's easy availability has sometimes created ignorance to the magick it holds, sometimes merely looking at it as a "cooking herb", though much like anything in our tradition, we look beyond the obvious and commune with the spirit of the plant.

To understand what this herb entails, we must travel back to its folklore. Basil is said to be Greek, coming from the word basilikon, meaning "king" for its crown-shaped crest, though some believe the word stems from the mythological basilisk, a serpent that could kill with its lethal gaze. While the basilisk's venom was deadly, it was said that Basil leaves could cure against the look, the breath and even the bite of a basilisk. Modern day medicinal lore states that Basil will aid in venomous bites, drawing from the stories of these mythos.

An herb associated with the zodiacal sign of Scorpio, Basil was also associated with scorpions. Legend states that if you wanted to attract a scorpion, you would place Basil underneath a flowered pot and soon enough a scorpion would appear, drawing its lore back to the basilisk.

My relationship with Basil came from its energies of harmony and peace, blossoming into love and abundance. While growing up in an Hispanic household, we didn't use much (if any) Basil at all. I can recall the first time really tasting it and feeling a kinship begin with this plant spirit. Though it would take years for me to truly understand why we would feel drawn to each other, I could feel the essence of romance bloom in each dish it kissed. Basil was quick to instruct that I not "tear" the pieces when ingesting it, as it was tearing away the qualities it was born to share. Instead I was to chiffonade it (a cooking technique of stacking the herb's leaves, rolling them up and slicing them into thin strips, creating ribbons); it was a partnership – the leaf gifting its energies and qualities to my food, while I cared for it and tended to it, tending to its own personal funerary rite, preparing to honor its sacrifice so I could benefit from its teachings.

Traditionally the seeds and roots are rarely used, though in my meditations with Basil it spoke about the deeper lore of its root magick; how the roots would penetrate the soil, the body of the Earth, to birth and share its qualities. As the seeds are planted, the consecration of greenlore begins; when they first begin to sprout, its essence of purification is born; and as the roots spreads itself into the soil, so begins the fertility rites of the Earth.

To us, the heart of the magick and the herb is in the leaf and stem itself, though there is equal and profound magick found within the seeds and roots. Just as with most things, fresh is best. Its newness of life and visionary aid is ripe with power, channeling the best parts of the element of fire, our drive to be passionate, and to grow in all areas.

Fresh leaves, thinly sliced into strips, sprinkling them over nourishment, over self in sacred bath as ribbons, give way and meld with the purification of water splashing around you... its freshness purifying you, purifying your space, consecrating harmony within and without.

In its dried form, Basil is deeply concentrated. Its power has gone within, deep to the core of the herb, and its activation of these qualities is necessary to awaken the plant spirit. Place a dash or more into the palm of your hand, the map of your soul, and rub together, calling on its powers as the Bringer of Luck, the powers of transformation, guiding you in your visionary quest. Sprinkle it on your fire and call to the salamanders and the dragons. Seek to attune deeper with the mysteries of fire.

In the Hindu traditions, Basil is sacred to Vishnu and Krishna. Placed in Hindu homes, it serves as protection from all forms of evil. It is considered to be a form of Lakshmi, the Hindu goddess of abundance and prosperity. Basil kept and carried is known to bring luck and abundance to all who attune to it.

When speaking with Basil, I asked what its deepest message was to be shared, and it relayed:

Follow my dance into the deepest spirals of the Earth. Let my scent intoxicate you. Let my taste tickle you. I am the fusion of love of Self, and love of others. Luck and prosperity travel through the veins of my leaf... trace them, and my magick will emerge.

Horsetail

By Adam Sartwell

t all started with a tarot card at Samhain that I was given by one of the priests of the ritual. Going into the ritual, I was planning on not taking one. The work of the year or the lesson to be learned is represented by the card passed to you on that fateful night. Past years have left me gun-shy about taking one. Having had the Tower, the Three of Swords, and the Ten of Swords on different years, and having them play out, made me not want to take a card at all. But on that night, I was compelled by some strange force. My card this year was Temperance. This card that signifies inner balance and the art of being between worlds, but more importantly to this story, is the art of alchemy. My inner voice screamed out its name as I looked upon the card. "Alchemy is what you should endeavor to learn. Alchemy will bring you out of the plateau you have reached in your spiritual practice."

I started as a stranger to this art and science. Reading books and listening to my partner who had already started his quest of alchemy and its mysterious operations, I set out on my own quest. My partner had started a process to make seven special tinctures, called spagyric tinctures, that corresponded to the seven planets. These tinctures were made by alchemical processes to bring about an essence that would ignite that planet's energy within you and refine you as the essence was made. The alchemists believe that the process of doing the work of alchemy, brings you closer to your own divine essence.

The process is done in correspondence to the seven chakras in the body from root to crown and the seven planets. Some alchemists will do all the seven tinctures at once, but knowing how intense the process can be, I wanted to focus on one before I moved to another. I started with the root chakra, which is associated with the planetary energy of Saturn. The traditional plant used in this seven tincture process for Saturn's herb is Horsetail.

According to herbal lore, Horsetail has two magickal uses. Making a whistle out of horsetail grass will call snakes to you, as they are reportedly charmed by its sound. Fornication in a bedroom with horsetail present causes pregnancy. I have not tried either operation seeing as I have no love of snakes or desire for getting a woman pregnant! The strange coincidence of how Horsetail deals with snakes and women and my name, Adam, is not lost on me. Fertility and snakes are Horsetail's magickal associations, but its planetary energy is that of Saturn.

In the Qaballah, the sephira of Saturn, Binah, is a representation of the Goddess, bringing form to the force of Chokma with her wisdom. Snakes always seem to be wise or tricksters in the tales, don't they?

Medicinally, Horsetail is used as a diuretic (increasing the volume of urine excreted), a hemostatic (acting to arrest bleeding or hemorrhage), and as a vulnerary (used in healing or treating wounds.) It has been used to treat lung problems, internal bleeding, ulcers, water retention, and as a douche for excessive menstrual flow. Alchemists report that Horsetail has an effect on the Saturnine symptoms and diseases, issues associated with the root chakra, the bones, ligaments, and things that are solid or stiff in the body, as well as chronic issues of all kinds that fall under its rulership. I have witnessed the spagyric tincture used to heal a pained rib from an old injury with success. The spagyric becomes not only the power of the herb but is a fluid talisman of the planet it represents. I have made fluid condensers before but it does not hold a candle to the process of making the spagyric.

On top of the reasoning that I have given for my foray into alchemy, I have a knee that pains me every once in a while. This is one of the things a spagyric of Horsetail would be used for and I have been assured of this by a competent herbalist. The right knee symbolizes the work you do in life. My work has always been more stressful and straining to my knee at times. Yet another reason to embark on the journey with the spirit of Horsetail at my side.

I ordered the herb from a reputable organic supply co-op. The next Saturday after it came, I woke at dawn to make the tincture in the most powerful hour and day for Saturn. I gathered the high-proof alcohol, a mason jar, some Saran wrap, and the dry herb, and went to my altar. I prayed to Saturn and to all the gods and goddesses I work with to fill the tincture with the power of Saturn. The process of making the tincture is as, or more important than, the tincture itself because it is supposed to be a conversation between you and the Great Spirit. What you observe from the process can lead you to the issues you are working through with the planet, or about the state of what it rules in your life. I say this because as I sat in my circle, I couldn't remember how much herb I had to put into the jar for the tincture. I said to myself, I think I have to make it about two thirds full. Really, all you need to do for an effective tincture with a dried herb is only one third of the bottle. I took this as the universe telling me that I had a lot of work to do with Saturn. Saturn rules karma, so perhaps I have more to work through karmically then I knew. I poured the alcohol over the herb until the jar was almost full, then placed the Saran wrap over the mouth. Some believe if the tincture touches the metal, it loses some of its properties. Then I screwed on the metal lid.

Forty days is an alchemical month, which is how long I let the tincture steep. I shook it every day or so to make sure that the herbs had full saturation and didn't just settle. The process takes out the alchemical "mercury" from the plant and adds it to the "mercury" of the vodka spirits. During this time I prayed to the gods to bless it and the plant spirit of Horsetail to empower it. Finally when the forty days were done, I waited again for dawn on a Saturday to separate the plant matter (the "feces" in herbal terms) from the spirits. The tincture is now ready for the process that will change its composition to a spagyric.

Taking the plant matter of the Horsetail and placing it in a Pyrex dish, set fire to it while it is still wet with the alcohol that didn't filter out. I started the process inside, and burned the herbs until they wouldn't light any more. I remembered something about adding more alcohol to the mixture to help get the herbs to burn down until they are black. So I ran upstairs to the apothecary and grabbed some grain alcohol. I found a bottle with about a cup of grain alcohol in it and came back downstairs. I added a little to the mixture and relit the herbs. It didn't flame up like before, so I thought I should add a little more alcohol to make it burn faster. This, readers, is an example of what *not* to do! I poured grain alcohol onto the mixture not knowing that part of it was still burning with those sneaky blue flames. The whole thing exploded, knocking me back in surprise and shooting herbal feces out in all directions, completely covering the kitchen. Strangely enough, I laughed as I picked myself up of the floor. I checked to see if I had my eyebrows, and I still did. I then thought about my sleeping partners upstairs and how embarrassed and ashamed I would be when they found out I had blown up alchemy in the kitchen! I started to sweep up the mess I had made, resolving that I wouldn't tell them the extent of my amazing stupidity. I found comfort in a book on alchemy that said no alchemist worth his salt could say he had never had an accidental explosion.

As I had halfway covered up the evidence of my misadventure, my partners stirred and came down to see what stinky business I was up to. My alchemist boyfriend said I used too much herb in my tincture and that mine would take a lot more to burn down then his did when he had done the operation. He then advised me to put some grain alcohol in the feces to burn it, but I should do it outside so that I wouldn't set off the fire alarms. To my credit, I took this advice with a straight face. Then, as he noticed the herbal spillage from the explosion, I told him I had a small "accident". He found it interesting and told me about the conversation he had with the Great Spirit about my Saturn issues and how I should meditate on where I explode in the realm of Saturn. I thought about shame and karma. I thought about how I felt like I had too much stuff in our small house, and how I felt overwhelmed at work and in my ministry work.

After the herb had blackened, I ground it down in a mortar and pestle. The herb went back into the Pyrex dish and into the oven on the highest temp I could have it. It began to smoke within ten minutes. I took it out and divided it into two Pyrex dishes because it was so thick it was cooking down in a very smoky way, telling me that if I wanted to broil down my karma, I would have to break it down into workable chunks. Finally after twelve hours of stinking up the house, some of the plant matter turned gray. Really, alchemists are aiming for white, but gray is acceptable. This whole burning process is to purify the "salts" out of the plant matter. When done, you put the "salts" and the "mercury" back together so that the purified salt of the herb can dissolve in the solution of tincture. This dissolving can take forty days too, if you're really hard core. I am not so hard core, so I chose to do three weeks of this process. Three is a number that resonates with Saturn in Qaballah. When the dissolving is done, you strain the tincture through a coffee filter, taking out any dross left over. You can do the whole process of burning to ash and putting it back in to dissolve one more time, but I was sure I was done. I waited to start taking the tincture because it was right before my vacation, and I wasn't sure I was ready to deal with Saturnine issues on the vacation.

The next Saturday, I enacted a ritual to charge the tincture for the power of Saturn. The alchemists I have read about didn't all agree on whether or not this should be done or if it was necessary, but I thought it was a good way to start the process of taking it and awakening the herb spirit within it as well as the Saturnine energies.

This alchemical ritual is how I came to know the spirit of Horsetail, a plant I hardly knew existed. My alchemical journey taught me much about myself and my life and I will always have a special place in my heart for the power of Horsetail.

Lavender:
The Good Witches' Herb

By Carmen Reyes

Lavender

Lavandula angustifolia, L. officinalis, L. vera, L. spica, L. stoechas
Folk Names: Elf Leaf, Nardos, Spike
Common name: English Lavender
Parts used: Flowers
Planet: Balsamic and New Moon, Mercury, Saturn
Zodiac: Virgo
Tarot: The Hermit
Goddess: Hecate
Rune: Hagalaz
Animal: Snake

avender is a fragrant shrub indigenous to the mountainous areas of the Mediterranean. Found on sandy coastal soil or rocky places, this hardy perennial is cultivated the world over for its aromatic spikes of blue flowers. The whole plant is used commercially, but the violet flowers are valued for their essential oil. Various species of lavender are used in the preparation of the commercial essential oil, but most are obtained from the flowers of *Lavendula vera.* The most important varieties are spike lavender (*L. spica*), French lavender (*L. stoechas*), and true or English lavender (*L. officinalis*), also known as *L. angustifolia* and *L. vera.* *L. officinalis.* The true lavender is used medicinally while *L. spica,* known for its insect repelling abilities, is the variety the ancient Romans used to perfume their baths.

Lavender is a member of the Mint Family, *Labiateae,* also called *Lamiaceae,* a family of plants with squarish stalks and simple, opposite leaves. The flowers of this family are aromatic, bisexual, and irregular.

There are many forms of the prized lavender and all are medicinal and antiseptic. Considered stimulating due to its ability to increase circulation, it is a superb cleanser of the skin and body both internally and externally. Lavender is cooling, emotionally clearing, and used to bring sleep, relieve tension and nervous exhaustion.

It is one of the essential oils that can be applied to the skin (undiluted), and it is considered very safe for use, although caution should always be used with essential oils, and diluting with extra virgin olive oil is recommended.

Lore

As an herb, Lavender has been in documented use for over 2,500 years. People in India called it spikenard because of its spike shaped flowers and it was known by this name in biblical times, although spikenard is the name of a member of the Aralia family known as American Spikenard or Wild Sarsaparilla. The Greeks referred to it as Nardus after a Syrian city, and the Romans called it Lavender, possibly derived from the Latin verb "lavare" which means "to wash" or from the word "livendulo" which means "livid or bluish".

Although the first recorded cultivation of lavender was found to be by ancient Egyptians who used it to make healing ointments, perfume and balm for mummification, ancient Romans used lavender as a perfume for their hair and recognized it for its healing and antiseptic qualities. It was thought to restore the skin and was used lavishly in the bath. In preparation for childbirth it was used to keep away infection.

Lavender is dedicated to Hecate, Goddess of the Crossroads, protectress of birth, death, and guide to travelers.

A favorite strewing herb for floors of homes and churches during the Middles Ages, in the 16th century, lavender's antiseptic qualities were said to stave off the ravages of the plague. Wardrobes and cupboards revealed drawers of scented linens. Bundles were tied to wrists and French glove makers scented their leathers with its oil. As the plague swept through Toulouse, France in 1630, four thieves gained notoriety through a mysterious recipe now called "Four Thieves Vinegar," (*Vinaigre des Quatre Voleurs*). The formula containing thyme, lavender, rosemary and sage steeped in vinegar, became a cure all in the 19th century with the addition of garlic.

Throughout history, lavender has symbolized purity, protection, and healing. Lavender's ability to purify the body and spirit of physical and energetic "negatives" has placed it atop the list of beneficial plants. Lavender can be used fresh, dried, distilled, infused, and is an ingredient in foodstuffs including cookies, cakes, icing, ice cream, and chocolate. It is prepared as an essential oil, massage oil, perfume, cream, ointment, inhalation, tincture, dry herb, or fresh as tea, bath, and floral water.

Uses

Inhale

Place one drop of essential oil on one hand, rub palms together, cup the hands placing thumbs together and inhale to enliven the senses and invite peacefulness.

Unguent

In sacred space, make an unguent (ointment imbued with spiritual energy and used for ritual purposes or one containing a medicinal ingredient) by combining a small amount of unrefined shea butter with a drop or two of *L. vera*.

Recipe: 10–15 drops per 2 ounces shea butter. This can be used to massage temples to relieve tension and clear unwanted thoughts as well as applied to wrists as a calming perfume

Flower Essence

Lavenger is a visionary herb that balances the emotions and can enhance the effects of the herbal remedy when taken internally. Lavender supports the flow of vibrational energy, stimulates the sixth chakra, for clear vision and removes blockages to spiritual growth. It is a fine essence to accompany divination, taken directly from the bottle or diluted in water. You can enhance a bath with 5–10 drops of flower essence. Bathe on the Balsamic Moon to let go of the old.

Floral Water

Lavender hydrosol, obtained by steam distillation is refreshing and evocative of childhood memories. Spray the hydrosol full strength on linens or pillows for a fresh clean scent in preparation for dream work. For calming or to encourage sleep, spray the nape of neck.

It can be used full strength or diluted with pure water in a spray bottle as a personal purifier before ritual work or divination.

Holy or Lustral Water

As an herb of consecration that blesses and removes unwanted energies, Lavender as a hydrosol can be used undiluted or diluted to make an essence that purifies. Add several drops to pure water in a glass bowl, recite incantations, invocations or prayers over the water to imbue it with spiritual intent. Then asperge (from Latin asperses, to scatter and to sprinkle with water) your inner and outer temple by dipping whole lavender stalks with flowers into the water, focusing on the directions of your space, and head to toe for yourself.

Bath

Run hot bath water over a tied closed muslin bag containing several handfuls of dried lavender flowers to soothe and unwind. It is recommended to use dried plant in the bath rather than the pure essential oil as dispersing the oil can be a bit tricky causing an unpleasant experience for some.

Florecidas

A Mayan spiritual bath is a great way to start the day. Fresh flowers are used for this bath that traditional healers administer to patients for cleansing of the spiritual body. Focus your intention on purifying and gratitude to the Lavender spirit the moment you set out to gather fresh flowers. Plants used for spiritual bathing must be collected with prayer and care. I recite an adaptation of The Herb Collector's Prayer: "In the name of the Goddess Hebe, Hera, Hecate, I give thanks to the spirit of this plant and I have faith with all my heart that you will help me to make a healing, purifying bath for (person's name)."

Note: Always use lavender that is grown without chemicals or pesticides, certified organic dried herb, essential oil, and flower water hydrosol or flower essence as commercial plants tend to accumulate toxic agricultural and environmental pollutants. The essential oil is potent and not to be taken internally without qualified practitioner supervision.

Divination

Try a lavender divination at bedtime by placing a small handful of flowers inside your pillowcase to connect with ancestral memory and receive divine messages. Keep a journal by your bedside and note ideas that emerge upon waking.

Spell

Lavender in any form may be used in as an ingredient for spells and formulas relating to the domain of Mercury: mental outlook, nervous exhaustion, spiritual guidance, wisdom, communication, divination, self-improvement, and intellectual endeavors. "Despite lavender's mercurial nature, it is believed capable of invoking Deities such as Hecate and Saturn" for works requiring permanence, and protection from the evil eye.

Symbolism

The tarot image of the Hermit atop a high cliff revealing a golden light brings to mind an image of Hecate with her torches lighting the Underworld. Ruled by Mercury, Virgo is the discriminating intellect, ever busy purifying and improving the self, the home, and temple. Since ancient times, snakes have been a symbol of wisdom, healing, and flowing energy as represented by the caduceus, a symbol of medicine. The rune association is Hagalaz, the seed rune representing disruptive forces, changes in consciousness, the element of fate, and the Goddess Hella. Hella, Hel, or Holda, Goddess of the Underworld and The Wild Hunt, is a Northern counterpart to the Roman Goddess Hecate. During the Balsamic Moon, ritual banishing is appropriate. The New Moon is a time of new beginnings, a time to plant seeds, and to cleanse in preparation of new works.

Lavender Invocation

Lavandula vera
Lavare
Unctio
Verto

This Latin invocation calls to the lavender spirit asking for its power for your magical working. Lavare means to wash, Unctio, to anoint, and Verto, to transform.

The translation is Lavender spirit, wash me, anoint me, and transform me.

Sources

Arvigo, Rosita. *Spiritual Bathing.* Berkeley, CA: Celestial Arts, 2003.

Bereyl, Paul. *A Compendium of Herbal Magick.* Blaine, WA: Phoenix Publishing, 1998.

Cech, Richo. *Making Plant Medicine.* Williams, OR: Horizon Herbs, 2000.

Culpepper, Nicholas. *Culpepper's Complete Herbal.* UK: Wordsworth Editions, 1995.

——.Culpepper's Complete Herbal, *http://www.complete-herbal.com/details/lavender.html* (Accessed 3/28/2011).

Scott. *Cunningham's Encyclopedia of Magical Herbs.* Woodbury, Minnestoa: Llewellyn Publications, 2005.

Elpel, Thomas J. *Botany in a Day.* Pony, Montana: Hops Press, 2004.

Holmes, Peter. *The Energetics of Western Herbs,* Vol. 2. Boulder, CO: Snow Lotus Press, 2006.

Lust, John. *The Herb Book.* NY: Bantam Books, 1974.

Kaminski, Patricia and Katz, Richard. *Flower Essence Repertory.* Nevada City, CA: the Flower Essence Society, 2004.

McIntyre, Anne. *Flower Power.* NY: Henry Holt, 1996.

Mojay, Gabriel. *Aromatherapy for Healing the Spirit.* Rochester, VT: Healing Arts Press, 1997.

Supplies

FES Lavender, *Lavandula officinalis* flower essence 0.25 oz. available from Flower Essence Services *www.fesflowers.com*

Organic lavender Lavandula spp. flower, raw unrefined shea butter, organic lavender hydrosol (Origin: Bulgaria), organic lavender lavandula angustifolia essential oil (Origin: Ukraine) from Mountain Rose Herbs *www.mountainroseherbs.com*

Organic Lavender Highland, Lavandula vera essential oil 5 or 10ml cobalt bottle, Lavandula vera hydrosol 30ml cobalt spray bottle from Oshadhi *www.oshadhiusa.com*

The Magick of Lemon Balm

By Christopher Penczak

hen I began my herbal training, one plant in the garden came back to me time and again, Lemon Balm. While there were certainly more flashy flowers and plants looming tall, and those with greater magickal lore, it was Lemon Balm that caught my attention. Square stemmed member of the mint family, Lamiaceae, unlike traditional mints, it smells of citrus, specifically lemon. It's amazing how many plans smell like the lemon – Lemon Grass and Lemon Verbena as two of the most prominent, but Lemon Balm has a special magick.

Lemon Balm's plant spirit is known as a helper, an aid. Her Latin name, Melissa officinalis, is named after the honey bee in Greek, Melissa, as it attracts bees. But Melissa is also a term for a priestess who assists the oracle priestesses. Many great goddesses are considered to be "Queen Bees" and are attended by priestesses considered to be "bees" or "melissa." Lemon Balm's spirit is like an attending priestess, willing to aid and help us in whatever ways are necessary. Three "Bee Goddesses" known as the Thirae, gave Apollo his gift of prophecy. It is excellent to work with bees directly, around hives, as it can produce a large amount of nectar for the bee, despite its small size, and as offering to "bee goddesses," and deities of prophecy.

Herbally, Lemon Balm is a tonic. While it doesn't have a strong chemical action, it grants great benefit over time. It is said to sooth an upset stomach and calm the nerves, though it's not a sedative or nervine. It can help you sleep. It helps improve digestion and balance your systems. It helps deal with stress and tensions. Those who suffer from vertigo can be aided with Lemon Balm. Modern research indicates it also has some antiviral and antimicrobial features, and has a high antioxidant content. Lemon Balm makes a good addition to any tea or tincture for colds and flus. It is also used in mouthwash and toothpastes, and a wide variety of medical cordials and waters. It is often part of the absinthe formula of the famous Green Fairy liquor, as well as Benedictine and Chartreuse. There is also some evidence to show it can inhibit the thyroid, making it useful in hyperthyroid conditions, but can also inhibit certain thyroid medications.

One of its classic names is the "Herb of Good Cheer" like a good friend, cheering us up from difficulties and bringing optimism and light into any situation. It is said to chase away sadness. It appears by some to be a "heal all" for some herbalists, as it is used in a wide range of herbal tonics. Stress, tension, depression, and poor digestion are a source of some illnesses.

Lemon Balm tea and tincture has been a greater healer for me personally. As someone who travels and deals with the public a lot, I take Lemon Balm religiously when on tour or when having a heavy teaching schedule. It helps me keep in "good cheer" when dealing with people, and dealing with the stresses and strains of travel.

Alchemists would say that Lemon Balm is one of the premiere herbs of life force. This humble herb is said to store more life force, more prana, than other herbs. Some attribute it with extending the life and increasing overall energetic balance. Melissa is used in a specially prepared alchemical tincture, known as an Ens tincture, specifically an Ens of Melissa as documented by the alchemist Paracelsus. Paracelsus considered Lemon Balm elixir the source of life.

The Entia (plural of Ens), according to Paracelsus, are sources of influence, be they physical, psychic, or spiritual, that can be the source of illness. He named five:

1. *Ens Astrorum or Ens Astrale* – the astrology of the patient, both natal and influencing transits that can be attributed to illness and weakness.

Lemon Balm

2. *Ens Veneni* – the toxins accumulated in the body from the environment.
3. *Ens Naturale* – the general physical constitution and health, or lack thereof.
4. *Ens Spirituale* – illness caused by spirits and entities.
5. *Ens Dei* – the illnesses decreed by the Will of God. While the first four can be aided and improved on by Ens tinctures and alchemical medicines, the fifth was only curable through the Will of God.

The Ens of Melissa is difficult to prepare, though the properties attributed to it include total physical regeneration. It is the first of the Ens tinctures to be made. Alchemists report finding the properties so startling, they gave it to chickens while soaking kernels of grain in it. The old, eggless chickens reportedly lost all their feathers which grew back healthy and whole, and the chickens started to lay eggs again. The Ens of Melissa is made with the following:

Start by making Angel Water, also known as the Oil of Tartar. Angel Water is water infused with vital life force, or the "Secret Fire" of the alchemists, through the use of plant salts. It forms of the basis of Ens tinctures and other alchemical preparations.

Take plant ashes (wood ashes such as oak are ideal, as they contain Potassium Carbonate) and soak them in large pot of filtered rain water. Use goggles and gloves, as the mixture is caustic. Use twenty times the water to the volume of ash. Boil the mixture for twenty minutes and filter into a large pan. Evaporate the liquid, leaving the trace salts.

Grind the salts and calcinate, or heat, the salt in a heat proof dish at 500 degrees C. Cool the salts and repeat the process, dissolving them again in rain water. Many will repeat the "wash" process several times to get the purest salts. Repeat this process until you have two cups of dry salt, also known as potash. Those who don't want to go through this process will simply purchase potash (Potassium carbonate) though the true alchemist believes you must make your own to be connected to the vegetable realm. In alchemy, these salts are called the Salt of Tartar.

In the spring, when the Sun is in Aries, Taurus, or Gemini, when the Moon is waxing, spread this salt out thin upon a glass dish in the late evening. Place the dish outside in nature, but above the ground. I put it on wooded blocks. At sunrise, collect the dish, which should be filled with water. This is the Oil of Tartar. The salts act as a "magnet" for the life force. Again, you should be using goggles and gloves, as the mixture is caustic and will etch glass. Traditionally using distilling equipment made from glass, not metal, distill off the liquid and leave the salt behind. The liquid is now known as filtered Angel Water. You can save the salt and use it for repeated work, washing it out of the distilling equipment, evaporated and saved for future use. Unfiltered Angel Water can be used in the preparation of Ens Tinctures. Unfiltered angel water should not be used topically or internally.

Take a few ounces of dry Lemon Balm herb and cover it with unfiltered Angel Water (Dew Water and Plant Salt). Remember, it will etch glass and is toxic. Pour an equal amount of grain alcohol into the mix. Shake daily, allowing the two to mix regularly. The alcohol will take the color of the Angel Water/Oil of Tartar, but only through repeated mixing. The life force "rises" up to the alcohol. When the alcohol on the top layer takes the color of the Oil of Tartar, pipette off the alcohol, being sure not to take any of the caustic Oil of Tartar with it.

To consume the Ens tincture, take 10-20 drops in water or wine. Generally one takes it on the planetary day associated with the herb. Since alchemists more often associate Lemon Balm with Jupiter, it is best taken on a Thursday, but for the healing of chronic conditions, take it daily for forty days. It is also particularly powerful to take prior to any magick or meditation involving Jupiter, including Qabalistic pathworkings involving Chesed, the sphere of Jupiter, or Wheel of Fortune, ruled by Jupiter. Ens tinctures are considered "initiatic" products, making profound changes in the body, mind, and soul of the person consuming them, much like an initiation ritual and infusion of energy from a tradition.

The flower essence of Lemon Balm is a bit easier to make and obtain. Its nature embodies the supportive quality of Melissa. It lightens the situation of anyone taking it. It provides nurturing and support, helping to relieve stress. Think of how the scent of lemon just refreshes and uplifts. It's one of the reasons why the lemon scent is used to clear and clean a space. Our use of lemon scent in American cleaning products comes from the use of Lemon Grass in Hoodoo floor washes, but Lemon Balm has a similar effect. It is added to dosage bottles of intense flower essences, to help the client keep humor and perspective, and appreciate the little things while going through difficult healing.

In magick and alchemy, Lemon Balm is associated with Venus, Jupiter, and the Moon. It can be used in love and beauty magick, particularly in bath water or a face wash. Make Lemon Balm tea by steeping one tablespoon of dried herb to a cup of hot water and add to bath water. To use as a face wash, let the water cool, soak a face cloth in it, and wash the face. Carried in a pink or green charm bag, lemon balm can attract a lover to you. The tea can also be drunk to sooth the heart when experiencing a break up. This helps soothe our sadness. It is also said to help communication between lovers in general, and particularly when having a quarrel.

Jupiter associations come with the qualities of expansive and uplifting life force. It can be used in all manner of healing spells and potions. While not specifically a money herb, its helpful nature can be useful when doing any type of money or business magick, giving a supportive and optimistic attitude about the situation, and because of this, it is also used in manifestation spells.

Lemon Balm is associated with prophecy and prophets, and can be used in psychic spells to increase awareness and the ability to communicate these intuitions to others. It helps support other visionary herbs, such as Mugwort. Due to its mild tranquilizing properties, easing stress, it can be used in dream sachets for prophetic dreams, or drunk as a tea before bed for the same reason.

I've found that a little Lemon Balm added to any spell helps the success of the spell. She is my ally and my helper. She is very gregarious. Because we have that relationship, we can work together in a wide range of magicks. I encourage all magicians to seek out the help and counsel of Melissa, and find a willing partner ready to aid you in all of your desires.

The Song of Mint

By Angela Pote

he song of mint. She has lasted through the time of mythology and has traveled the world. Her song is low into the depths of our roots and as high as the air that blows. Mentha is her name and a sad song she sang. Mentha was a nymph in Greece who loved Hades and he fell in love with her as well. When Persephone, Hades's wife, found out, she became jealous and cursed Mentha to be a lowly plant to grow close to the earth, so she would be trampled on by all who passed. Hades, not being able to undo the spell, cast one of his own. He gave Mentha a sweet fragrance so he could still cherish her when he walked by.

The Description of Mint

— from *botanical.com*

From creeping roots-stocks, erect, square stems rise to a height of about two feet, bearing very short-stalked, acute-pointed, lace-shaped, wrinkled, bright green leaves, with finely toothed edges, and smooth surfaces, the ribs very prominent beneath. The small flowers are densely arranged in whorls or rings in the axils of the upper leaves, forming cylindrical, slender tapering spikes, pinkish or lilac in color. The little labiates flowers are followed by very few, roundish, minute brown seeds. The taste and odor of the plant is very characteristic.

There are several forms of Garden Mint, the true variety being of bold, upright growth, with fairly large and broad leaves, pointed and sharply serrated (or toothed) at the edges and of a rich, bright, green color. Another variety, sometimes sold as Spearmint (M. cardiaca), is much smaller and less erect in growth, with darker leaves, the whorls of flowers distant and leafy, but possessing the same odor and flavor, and another has comparatively large, broad or rounded leaves. Yet another has soft hairs, but this, though distinct from what is known as Horse Mint, is inferior to the true Spearmint.

A form with its leaves slightly crisped is common in gardens under the name of M. crispa.

The Three "M's" of Mint

Although she now bears many names Mentha Spicata is Spearmint and is used in many ways from medicinal to the main plate for many meals. Mint is used in magic as well. Mint is used both homeopathically and medicinally. Menthol, a compound obtained from Mint oils, is used in patches to reduce inflammation. Mint oils can be rubbed on sore or sprained muscles. These oils are also used to flavor what otherwise would be horrible tasting elixirs' and cough drops, and also aids the belly with the digesting of such medicines. Mint can be used alone in teas or with other herbs and fruits. I particularly like Mint with Star Anise and honey after a heavy meal to help with digestion and relaxation. Mint mixed with warm milk relieves stomach aches. My Grandmother would treat a baby with colic by boiling mint leaves and fennel seeds until the water would just start to turn yellow then strain it, add a little bit of sugar and give it to the baby. It is not advised to give a baby under two years of age honey, so Gram would just add sugar and the results were awesome. She would also give the mommy a spoon of Mint leaves after they were steeped and would say that it would heal both of them. Mint has a calming affect and considering by the time a colicky baby came around, the mommy would be a bit frazzled as well, that made sense.

If you have areas of patchy dry skin you can use olive oil and Mint infusion to rub on the patches once a day, to every other day for relief and aid in healing, Mint tea drunk at the times of monthly cramping will help relieve those pains.

To keep your youth, take a handful of Mint leaves with stems, squeeze them just a bit, add them to ice water, and let stand till it's at room temperature. Then, after a normal wash, take the Mint water and rinse your face.

Place mint, lavender, and salt in bathwater to have a relaxing night's sleep. It is also said that Mint aids one in keeping their memories. To help a little one sleep, make a small pillow with rice, mint, lavender, and star anise. When it's time for bed, place the pillow in the microwave for 30 seconds to one minute max. (Be extremely careful not to overheat. It can burn.) Place the pillow near the child and the aromas will guide them to rest. I place the pillows on a night stand near the crib; I have used them for all ages.

Mint in food is a cooling and refreshing way to rest the body and mind in the long hot summer nights, and in the cold brisk weather of winter, Mint will warm your soul. I could not even begin to imagine how many recipes there are for the use of mint within the culinary world, so here are just a few simple ones with nourishing the soul in mind.

Minty Cocoa

(serves two) You need your favorite hot chocolate, whether from a package or scraped from the cocoa bar itself. Two cups of milk, 1 to 1 ½ tablespoons of fresh mint, or 1 to 1 ½ tablespoon of dried mint, cinnamon, and whipped cream or marshmallows

While warming the milk steep the mint. When hot, strain, then add chocolate mix and cinnamon. Top with whipped cream or marshmallows.

Mint & Ginger Tea

(Good to drink when you feel a cold knocking at your door.)

Two cups of water, 1 to 1 ½ table spoons of fresh mint, or 1 to 1 ½ table spoon of dried mint, sliced fresh ginger, ginger powder or instant ginger tea works just as well (ginger is a fire spice. I suggest using it to your liking). With the slices, I only use 3 to 4 with the powder and tea to the taste.

Steep the mint and ginger in hot water, remove after 5–10 minutes. However, if you leave it in the whole 10 minutes, I suggest using less ginger as it can become overpowering. Add sweetener to taste.

Minty Mango Salsa
(serves 10)

1 large ripe mango, peeled & diced, 1 medium, sweet red pepper, diced, 1 can (4 ounces) chopped green chilies, ¼ cup chopped red onions, 1 tablespoon lime juice, 1 tablespoon of lemon juice, 3 tablespoons minced fresh mint, ¼ teaspoon ground ginger

In a bowl, mix all the ingredients. Cover and refrigerate for 3 to 4 hours before serving. This can be enjoyed with tortilla chips or served over grilled pork.

Walla Mint Brownies

1 package of brownie mix, 3 bars of mint chocolate candy, 1/3 cup of walnuts, for garnish (optional)

Prepare brownies according to directions. Break or chop the candy bars and add them to the mix. Bake accordingly. When done, top with walnuts and set out to cool.

How well does mint grow? In my experience, very well. It was the second plant that had ever survived my not so green thumb, and is now resting during the winter months. Mint is a perennial, preferring a moist heavy soil, but will grow and flourish in almost any soil. However it is difficult to grow in dry, sandy soils. It's not impossible, just difficult. I started with a very small mint plant and before I noticed it, she needed a bigger pot. When she could not spread out, she went up. When planting mint in a bed, use bricks or stone to contain her as she can get a little wild. It is best to try to plant in a place that receives both sun and shade during the day.

This brings me to Mint magic. Whatever we use Mint for within this world, we can mirror that into the magic world. As this plant has a "creeping root" she moves deep within the soil and grows very quickly. Mint helps with the inner parts of one's digestive system. Mint is an air herb and her smell travels through the air. Her fragrance can make one hungry for the sweetness within. The watery crispness of Mint cleanses the palette, and so can cleanse the soul. Mint can be used in helping your root chakra open or to stay open, also helping one stay rooted, as she knows how to grow in any soil. So if you feel like you're going to fly away, take a ritual bath with mint and have a cup of mint tea. Mint helps with the inner parts of one's digestive system (the places that no one sees and no one can get to) and her gentleness can help with those parts of us. When things get crazy and you're battling the inside of yourself, snack on fresh mint and let her oils cool you down. The smell of Mint is just fabulous as she travels through the air. I use mint to aid in astral travel along with some sandalwood and frankincense mixed and burned over coals. Use mint in petition spells. You can infuse mint with water and sprinkle it on your petition. I put some on my fingers and rub the corners or the paper. I have even used mint extract in a jam. Mint placed near outside doors is said to drive mischievous spirits away. Mix mint in water and cleanse your home to get rid of negativity. The types of spells you can use mint for are enormous. The last two spells I will give you are fire, air, water, and earth spells. Each ingredient holds one of the elements and all can be used in any type of love spell. I use this for balancing my love as well as my significant other. You know those times when you just feel like you're at each other's neck but you don't know why? This spell brings balance that will help the both of you come back to your center.

Balancing Love

6 teaspoons each of cinnamon, mint, henbane, cinquefoil (separate in half), 2 green sachets, 1 item each from you and your partner, small picture, and two strands of hair (one from each partner).

In one sachet, place 3 teaspoons of each herb and add your personal item. Then, do the same to the next sachet putting in your partner's item. The sachet with your partner's item is what you will carry, and they will carry yours for 6-9 days. Only on the 6th or the 9th day, take both bags and bury them on your property or if you cannot do that you can bury them in a flower pot. I have even emptied the items and mixed them together and burned them over coals and thanked the herbs for bringing us back to the center. You can also infuse this mixture with oil (not the picture) and dress a candle or two for a special night.

When I did a meditation with Mint not so long ago, she sang me a song, one that helped me see how beautiful she is and how much she wants to help us. Mint is a soul that has overcome and can help us do so as well. She knows the heart and can navigate it, and can fly through the air like a dove. Her song is sweet and her touch is soft so open your heart and hear her song and soon you will sing along with her.

Ode to Mugwort

By Karen Charboneau-Harrison

Mugwort, Moxa, Traveler's Herb, Artemis Herb, Felon Herb, Muggons, Old Man, Sailor's Tobacco. Cingulum Sancti Johannis AKA St. John's plant (*not* St. John's Wort), Mother of Herbs, Mater Herbarum

oftly luminescent under the light of the full moon, Mugwort (*Artemisia vulgaris*) is truly a lunar herb. Mugwort is considered a sacred herb of Artemis, the Greek goddess of the moon, the hunt and chastity, hence its scientific Latin name. Amazing in its multiplicity of uses, both magickal and medicinal, Mugwort can be used in cooking, burned in an incense, as a smudge, as a 'moxa', smoked to induce mild intoxication, placed in a dream pillow, added to the bath.... the list goes on. In whatever manner one chooses to employ this versatile herb, it relaxes the body, balances the human system and allows one's inner sight and intuition to awaken.

Mugwort is a single-stemmed plant with drooping, elongated, oval shaped, 2 to 4 inch long leaves. These leaves are deeply toothed and pointed with green tops and silver white fuzz on the bottom. The plant grows as high as 6 feet with a width of 1 to 2 feet. Its flowers cluster on the stem tips and are tiny, reddish-brown and wooly. Mugwort blooms from July to August and is native to both Europe and Asia. It was brought to the United States from Europe and now grows wild across most parts of the country. This hardy plant is easy to cultivate and grow in your own backyard. If you wish to grow Mugwort from seed, it will germinate in 10-24 days. Start your seeds indoors in small Dixie cups or an egg carton. Once the plants are about 6 inches tall, plant them outside after Mother's Day, spacing each plant 8 to 12 inches apart in a place that will receive full sun. In a moist garden, Mugwort will spread itself rapidly by runners.

Lore has it that the word Mugwort is derived from the word "mug" because the herb was used in flavoring drinks, and, indeed, people were still flavoring their home-brewed beer with this worthy herb well into the 19th century in England and Germany. It is also possible that Mugwort is derived from the old Norse "muggi", meaning marsh, and the Germanic word "wuertz", meaning "root", which refers to its use since ancient times to repel insects - particularly moths. One of the 9 healing herbs of the Anglo-Saxons, it has been used throughout the Middle Ages, and into modern times for magick and for healing. Although Chinese healers and medieval European practitioners used Mugwort almost exclusively as a woman's remedy to increase fertility, ease birth, stimulate the elimination of the placenta and afterbirth, alleviate menstrual pains and balance menstrual irregularities, in Russia its properties were traditionally extracted into vodka as a tincture for easing arthritis, reducing swelling, cleaning wounds, and alleviating various skin problems.

Mugwort has a multitude of medicinal uses. It is a valuable digestive and tonic herb and can improve the appetite and digestive functions. It promotes liver detoxification and aids the body in the absorption of nutrients as well as increasing bile flow. Mugwort encourages the elimination of worms, is an antiseptic and can be used in the treatment of malaria. While it has long been used in the West to promote menstruation, in Chinese formulas it is prescribed as an infusion to prevent miscarriage, leading one to the realization that Mugwort helps to balance the female reproductive system as a whole. Using a Mugwort tea or compress during childbirth helps to speed labor and help expel the afterbirth. Mugwort is valuable in decreasing external inflammation from wounds or insect bites and, in both the East and the West, a poultice is traditionally placed on areas where there is rheumatic and arthritic pain.

In Asia, the Chinese use their native Mugwort (*Ai Ye*) in a tea for nausea and lower abdominal pain as well. It is commonly used as a 'moxa' by rolling the fuzzy leaves into moxa cones for use in acupuncture treatments that penetrate the body with heat rather than the acupuncture needletip. This treatment is called 'moxification' or 'moxibustion' - the moxa is ignited and due to its heat conductivity and gentle warmth, the smoldering herb transfers heat into the body's meridians by placing the moxa heated needle onto the surface of the skin.

Mugwort for Healing and Household Uses

For a Tincture

Place Mugwort leaves (dried or fresh) in grain alcohol or vodka. Fill a small, dark, wide-mouthed jar (such as a mason canning jar) halfway with the crushed Mugwort leaves. Cover the herb with the alcohol, close the jar, and let it steep for 2 to 3 weeks, shaking it vigorously once a day. Strain the tincture into dark dropper bottles to store. A daily dose is 3 to 5 drops administered 3 times daily. Take for menstrual pain, scanty menstruation, or prolonged menstrual bleeding. For use with childbirth, administer orally in prolonged labor to strengthen uterine contractions and to help expel a retained placenta. You can also use a Mugwort tincture as a stimulant and tonic for liver stagnation and poor digestion.

Mugwort Massage Oil

Fill a wide-mouthed jar with chopped, fresh Mugwort leaves, flowers, and roots. Add a carrier oil such as sunflower or sweet almond oil to cover the plant matter and close the jar. Place it in a warm, sunny spot for 2 to 3 weeks, then strain the oil into another jar (cheese cloth or panty hose work great for this!), adding 15 drops or so of essential oil of pinyon pine or birch for every pint Mugwortof Mugwort extracted carrier oil. Shake the mixture well before transferring it to amber or cobalt blue bottles. This oil makes an excellent rub for swollen, tired feet and for sore, strained or tense muscles.

Household

Long used to repel insects, you can simply hang the fresh cut plant in rooms around the home to repel moths and flies. Make a tea or infusion with Mugwort and then apply the tea directly to your skin on a camping trip to repel bugs. Place sachets of Mugwort leaves in closets or bureau drawers to keep moths away from your clothes.

Mugwort Sleeping Pillow

If you or your child has trouble with nightmares or insomnia, make a pillow of dried Mugwort flowers and leaves. Place the herb in a drawstring pouch made of a loosely woven fabric such as cheesecloth or muslin, or create a 'tussie' from loose-weave fabric by cutting an 8- or 10-inch square piece, placing a cup of the herb in the center of the fabric then bringing the fabric corners together crosswise. Twist and tie with a ribbon to contain the herb inside.

Mugwort for Psychic Development and Magick:

As an herb ruled by the moon, Mugwort strengthens and enhances the receptive quality of one's subconscious mind and inner psyche, resulting in greater awareness of dreams and lucidity within the dream state. It also promotes communication between the subconscious and conscious minds, leading to insight about both one's mundane and one's spiritual life. The focused use of Mugwort in infusions, incense, and the bath can help in accessing guidance and direction from one's innate intuition as well connecting to the wisdom within the ethereal, intuitive world surrounding us.

Mugwort dream pillows and infusions have been used for centuries to induce dreams and visions, helping the individual to remember dreams, direct activity within the dream state and experience vivid prophetic dreams. You can make a dream pillow as directed above for the sleeping pillow. Then, add a few drops of Jasmine oil to the pillow. Place the pillow on the nightstand or under the main pillow on your bed before you retire. As you drift into sleep, consciously direct yourself to remember your dream and be sure to keep a journal and pen right by your bed so that you can jot down your memories as soon as you awaken. If you wish to work directly with your subconscious mind while sleeping to help yourself stop bad habits or to ingrain a new habit (the moon rules the subconscious where habits are stored), hold the pillow and breathe in the scent before drifting off to sleep while focusing on the work you want your subconscious mind to do as your body rests. If you are working to awaken your psychic abilities, a dream pillow can be very helpful. If you seek prophetic dreams, ask yourself the question for which you seek an answer to as you breathe in the scent of the pillow and then relax; drifting off to sleep. You may then dream about the situation that night or over the next night or two. You may also get your answer in a sudden psychic flash within the next few days during your waking life. Before you begin any sort of meditation or psychic work, you can breathe in the scent from your pillow to open and stimulate your psychic senses for a deeper experience.

Mugwort has also been used traditionally to help contact the astral realm or as an aid for astral projection and remote viewing. If this is your goal, you may burn Mugwort as an incense, drink a Mugwort infusion, anoint yourself with essential oil, or use a dream pillow as you begin your session.

If you are studying the art of scrying - the use of crystal balls, scrying mirrors, or divining through the use of tea leaves -

there are many ways to utilize Mugwort to enhance your work. Burn Mugwort as an incense or apply the oil to your third eye during your working. Activate, attune and cleanse your divination tools with a Mugwort infusion or simply wipe the fresh leaves on your scrying tools. You may wish to store your divination tools in a box in which you keep a Mugwort dream pillow to enhance their focus.

Mugwort is wonderful to use in creating and cleansing sacred space. You may burn the herb as incense, hang the fresh cut plant in your temple, or use Mugwort as a smudge. Smudge sticks are simple and fun to make: Harvest the stems from July to September when the plant is flowering. Cut your plants just above the ground, and then cut each plant into a 12 inch length. Hold two or three plants tightly together and, beginning at the bottom stems, gently wrap the leaves and flowers around each other while tying a medium width thread around the plant in an open 'X' pattern. Keep your thread taut to hold the plants together and finish by looping the thread several times around the end of the smudge. Then tie the thread off at the top end. Hang each fresh Mugwort smudge stick upside down to dry in a well-ventilated, shaded spot. After drying approximately three weeks, you will have smudge sticks for use in purifying the energy in your home, temple, or office.

If you wish to harvest your Mugwort in a loose, cut and dried, form to be used in your formulas, cut the plant stems as you would for the smudge sticks, but don't tie the plants together, simply hang each plant up to dry, allowing ample space between each plant for good drying ventilation. When the plants have dried completely (two to three weeks), strip the leaves and flowers from the stems, crush the plant material with your hands, and store the resulting loose herb in a cool, dark space in brown paper sacks.

Also used traditionally for protection, particularly from the spirit world, Mugwort can be used with focused will to open the psychic doorways to spirit communication, You can use this same focused intention to shut that door to the spirit world. Helpful in calming poltergeist phenomena and removing negative energy, it is one of the nine herbs invoked in the pagan Anglo-Saxon Nine Herbs Charm, recorded in the 10th Century in *The Lacnunga,* a collection of Anglo-Saxon medical texts and prayers, written primarily in Old English and Latin:

"Remember, Mugwort, what you made known,
What you arranged at the Great proclamation.
You were called Una, the oldest of herbs,
you have power against three and against thirty,
you have power against poison and against infection,
you have power against the loathsome foe roving through the land."

— *Nine Herbs Charm,* 10th century

Mugwort reveals its connection to the energies of the moon in its medicinal uses by the ways it creates balance and strength within the female reproductive system, its ability to help the body and mind relax into meditation and repose, and in its uses for digestion (the stomach, ruled by the astrological sign Cancer). This lunar connection is also highlighted by the ways it is employed in psychic development, astral projection, and dreamwork—all lunar activities.

Mugwort is so versatile and simple to grow; add Artemisia Vulgaris to your magickal garden and take advantage of its diverse gifts!

Sting and Strength: Sister Nettle

By Ruby Sara

... Do you see the stinging nettle which I hold in my hand? Quantities of the same sort grow round the cave in which you sleep, but none will be of any use to you unless they grow upon the graves in a churchyard. These you must gather even while they burn blisters on your hands. Break them to pieces with your hands and feet, and they will become flax, from which you must spin and weave eleven coats with long sleeves; if these are then thrown over the eleven swans, the spell will be broken. But remember, that from the moment you commence your task until it is finished, even should it occupy years of your life, you must not speak. The first word you utter will pierce through the hearts of your brothers like a deadly dagger. Their lives hang upon your tongue. Remember all I have told you." And as she finished speaking, she touched her hand lightly with the nettle, and a pain, as of burning fire, awoke Eliza.

– from *The Wild Swans,* by Hans Christian Andersen

n the scrub and the sacked scars of earth, the nettle grows. Bright, cheerful, and blazingly green, it invites the newcomer with a grin, daring us to reach out and brush its wide leaves. But, as any experienced woodman, herbalist, or hiker will tell you, that would be a mistake. For underneath its lovely leaves, the nettle harbors a wicked sting. And I'm pretty sure it cackles after it stings you.

Stinging nettles, also called common nettles, can be found all over North America, and are considered a nasty weed in many places. Tough, resilient, and enthusiastic, nettles spring up predominantly in places where the earth has been disturbed. They serve as a ready warning against hiking through the brush in shorts, as they harbor venom that injects into the skin of those hapless passersby who brush against the tiny needle-like stinging hairs (called trichomes) underneath the nettle's leaves. The word "nettle" itself comes from the Anglo-Saxon word "noedle," meaning "needle." The nettle's venom is a combination of different chemicals that create a burning and stinging sensation, redness, and tingling that can last for hours.

Despite this, however, nettles have been used for food, cloth fiber, and medicine for centuries. The center of the nettle stalk is a hard fiber that, after a retting process similar to that of linen thread (culled from the flax plant), can be woven into textiles. When dried, boiled, steamed, or otherwise cooked, nettle leaves lose their sting, and the result is a delicious vegetable that can be eaten like spinach, dried and made into a tea or tincture, cooked into a variety of soups and other dishes, or made into nettle beer (though there are some brave souls who eat raw nettles competitively in the World Nettle Eating Championships in Dorset, it's not really a practice anyone actually recommends). And medicinally, nettles are a protein-rich powerhouse of nutritional value. They are rich in vitamins and minerals, and contemporary herbalists recommend nettles as an overall tonic herb, great for strengthening the body's overall system, and assuring strong and healthy bones, skin, hair, and nails. Nettles are also cleansing and detoxifying, and studies in Germany have found that in keeping with the teachings of folk medicine, nettles prove to be effective in treating inflammatory conditions such as arthritis.

Herbals are full of information about nettles – they've been used externally and internally for a number of ailments for centuries, and they even appear in the Anglo-Saxon Nine Herb Charm, said to be remedy for all known poisons:

"It is called nettle, it attacks against poison,
it drives off harmful things, casts out poison,

This is the plant that fought against the serpent,
This one has might against poison, it has might against infection
It has might against the evil that travels round the land."

Indeed, nettles are mean, yet proof against the evil and against mean creatures. They are the both/and, the hex and the heal, the sting and the strength. In Hans Christian Andersen's fairy tale *The Wild Swans,* Eliza is set the grueling task of harvesting, crushing, and weaving nettle fiber into charmed shirts for her eleven bespelled brothers, making nettles both a trial and a means of liberation. It is said that nettles are easier to pick bare-handed if you grasp them firmly instead of gently. It is true that knowing how to approach nettles can make for a very different experience when working with them in the wild. Nettles require trust, bravery, and strength, and they reward in kind. They challenge. They teach. Susun Weed says that the nettle's lesson is in paying attention: "You humans do not seem to pay much attention. Do you think you can quiet yourself enough to pay attention to me?"

Yes. For like that exquisite messenger of the gods, the honeybee, there is much to learn from listening to stinging creatures.

It is morning in the summer garden in the heart of my heart. There are flax flowers clustered together near the edges of the walk. Their bright moth-light blooms like small lavender colored stars. White clematis vines curl like cats along the wooden fence. Somewhere unseen, there rests the boundaries of the garden, the moss-coat stone wall, and the hidden door with its rusty latch. But here, the green ghosts of my blood speak to the hollow of me. And it is beautiful...manicured... perfect. (Here, the buttery petals of the hyacinth and the rich sweetness of the narcissus, their thornless stems smooth and slight as pencils...sweet green fuses.) And deeper still, almost within the heart of the garden, are the roses. Their fragile teacup scent dropping to the ground in a shower of petals like rain, some the size of my hands and others the size of lake pebbles. Yes, the crabapple blossoms and the irises, the lavender and the rosemary, and the honeybees humming among them all.

Yet here in the middle, here in the very center...the cultivated poetry of my garden heart fades into wilderness, and the scrub rises. The voice of my sister moves among the weeds. Sister nettle at the heart of my heart. Writing rough poems of dirt and venom, of sting and strength – the music on which the rest of my garden grows. Yes, the silver bells and cockleshells and the pretty nettle sisters...all in a row. Sister nettle sits in the heart of my heart, and sings.

I can't remember how old I was the first time I heard the story of *The Wild Swans*. Ten? Eleven? No matter the age, it remains one of the most profoundly enduring fairy tales of my life. And for all that it is long and beautifully imagined, two images stay with me to this day. The first is that of the single white rose that appears to declare Eliza's innocence just before she is burned for being a witch, and the other is that of young Eliza crushing stinging nettles with her bare feet, her hands raw from weaving the fiber into harsh shirts for her swan brothers. I didn't know what nettles were at the time I first encountered the story, I only knew they stung, and that Eliza's silent bravery seemed admirable...that if justice could not be satisfied, then at least something might be done. Work could be done by human hands that might lead to liberation, if not revenge. Eliza's image was with me the first day I tasted nettle tea, and the first day I brewed nettle beer. I learned to love their sly jokes, the glowing emerald green of new nettle shoots in spring (early leaves are much preferred to later plants...some recommend avoiding the ingestion of nettles after they've gone to flower), the rough papery sound of the leaves as they brushed against each other in my gathering sack.

I am not Eliza. I have no brothers, and certainly no brothers who live half their lives as swans. No fiery woman full of magic instructs me to pluck plants out of graveyards. There is no makeshift loom on which I silently weave. Yet, like Eliza, I too have come into relationship with the wicked sting of the nettle, and strive to understand its silent lesson.

Hex and heal. Sting and strength.
Sister nettle sits in the heart of a witch's garden.
And sings.

Care of Your Magickal Orchid

By Leslie Hugo

erhaps you have owned an orchid, or seen them in stores and thought they were too difficult to grow. With a little patience and understanding, growing an orchid is very easy, and your orchid will provide beauty and love for you and your home for many years.

Orchids are amazing plants. There are over 20,000 species of orchids on the planet, more species than any other form of life on the planet! They can be found in almost every country, and in most cultures, the orchid is a symbol of beauty. In my experience, beauty and love are the magick orchids provide. They can help you to find your inner beauty and love yourself, or they can bring beauty and love into the space that they grow. I have found that these qualities can be obtained in several ways. The first is through quiet meditation with your orchid. Let it speak to you, sending you images and messages. If you are not able to grow an orchid in your home or workplace, try taking an orchid flower essence. These can be purchased commercially, or made at home. You can even hang a picture of an orchid in your room or office, and meditate with the spirit of the plant.

When growing an orchid, it helps to have a little understanding of where and how they grow in nature. Most orchids are epiphytic, meaning that they grow on trees. They receive strong, but not direct sunlight, since they are shaded by the tree's leaves. They receive water from periodic rainfall, but the water runs off them and they can dry out. Being off the ground, they receive good air flow to their roots. It is these conditions that we try to create for them when growing them in our homes.

Phalaenopsis and *Paphiopedilum* orchids are easy to grow in your home if you have never owned an orchid. These are typically the kinds found in many grocery and home repair stores. When caring for your orchid, water it once a week by soaking it in room temperature water for about five minutes, then let it drain completely. Over watering is the leading cause of orchid death. Every other week, I add a very weak orchid fertilizer to my water.

Your orchid should be potted in loose bark, pumice, charcoal, or sphagnum moss, so that the roots can breathe, in a container with holes in the bottom so that excess water can drain out. Orchid bark can be purchased at most nurseries or garden stores. Keep your orchid on a shelf or table near a window where it will get strong light, but not direct sun. If the plant is getting too much sun, brown spots will appear on the leaves, indicating the leaves are getting sun burnt.

I have found that east windows work best for me. If you need to grow in a west or south window, place a sheer shade over the window to provide filtered light for your orchid. If you need to grow your orchid in a north window, you may need to supplement the light using a "natural sunshine" fluorescent bulb.

Most likely, your orchid will have blooms on it when you purchase it. Once the flowers have died and fallen off the stem, wait until the stem turns brown and withers. Some orchids will take a break in blooming, and decide a month later to put some more flowers out from the same stem. When the stem finally dies, clip it off close to the leaves. Your friend is now taking a break. Most orchids bloom once a year, but a few will bloom twice each year if you are lucky. Sometimes, it takes them one to three years to become comfortable with their new home before they will bloom again , so be patient with your magickal friend!

If you have questions about your orchid, the American Orchid Society has local chapters around the world, with members who are always willing to help out someone with questions. Their main website is *www.aos.org*.

Plantain

By Raven Kaldera

I see him always by the roadside – first the small ribbed leaves, then the larger ones, then the little stem with its curved head of seeds. The Native Americans called him Snakeweed for the shape of that stem, and indeed he has been used for snakebite. He looks up at me with a sideways smile and a twinkle in his eye as he sits beside the road, then his gaze turns and he looks away to the road's bends and ends. He is always looking to the road, no matter where he is. This is a plant spirit that likes to move.

Grandfather Waybread is an ol' travelin' man. Lean and weathered, with a wide grin beneath his tattered moustache, clothes full of holes, and leathery bare feet, he knows every byway and roadside from Chicago to Philadelphia to Helheim. He is a whistling gypsy with rings in his ears and a scarf knotted around his neck, a singing friar on eternal pilgrimage, a wandering hobo camping in a woodshed. He has a special relationship with the rune Raido, and can be called upon to help when you're lost, as long as you're walking – he doesn't really understand vehicles much, and navigates you by the weeds on the roadside.

While he seems like a happy-go-lucky sort, don't underestimate his intelligence – this is one of the Nine Sacred Herbs, and Grandfather Waybread is the one who knows where everything is. If there's a where in existence, he's been there, and can give you advice. He watches the heroes go on their adventures, and shakes his head after them, knowing what they've forgotten to bring or look out for that will be their downfall. If he really likes them, after they've fallen, he may do the regeneration trick. He is a powerful ally for psychic journeyers, as his powers extend through many other worlds, as well as our own.

Plantain (*Plantago major*) has been known by names as diverse as Waybread, St. Patrick's Dock, Snakeweed, Snakebite, Rat's Tail, White Man's Footprint, Dead Man's Footprint, Slan-Lus, and Ripple Grass. He is a small plant with a rosette of ribbed, stringy leaves, so common to both country field and city sidewalk that no one notices him. Almost everyone has seen him, but he prefers to fly quietly under the radar, growing up through the cement cracks and slowly ambling down each street. His brother Rib-Leaf (*Plantago lanceolata*), a longer and pointier version of Waybread, has the same qualities but is more common in southerly areas. I am almost convinced that they are actually the same greenwight wearing a different coat.

Although I met Grandfather Waybread as male, I got the feeling that he used to appear more as female in the ancient past. Plant spirits can do that; not only do they appear differently to different people, they can change their nature over the centuries. In the Song of the Nine Sacred Herbs, Plantain is known as Wegbrade or Waybread, and his rhyme refers to him as wyrta modor. However it happened, it seems that he prefers appearing as male now, for some unknown reason; at least it is so for me and my friends.

Native to all parts of Europe, the humble Plantain was extremely valued as a cure-all that he was claimed by medieval herbalists to help everything from rabies to snakebite. Pliny claimed that boiling him in a pot with dead body parts would cause them to rejoin and reanimate. In the North, it was called "Dead Man's Footprint" and was said to lead the way to Helheim, the Land of the Dead. In modern Northern Tradition Paganism, Waybread is associated with the world of Helheim and its Queen, Hela; and especially with the Helvegr, the road which the Dead walk to get to the great black gates of the Underworld. (His "snake" association makes sense here, as the snake tunnels down its own "road" to the lower worlds.) When

Waybread was brought to America, Native Americans began to call him "White Man's Footprint" as he got loose and became naturalized, which is an interesting twist on its other name.

Magically, Plantain leaves were bound to the head with red wool to cure headaches. Like Mugwort, it was placed in shoes to cure weariness on long trips. Waybread is a good travel-charm; hang it in your car to prevent evil from entering. Carrying the root supposedly protects from snakebite.

Shamanically, this is the plant of Helheim, the land of the Dead. His shamanic uses are many and varied and rather subtle; this lowly weed should not be underestimated. Remember, again, that he is one of the Nine Sacred Herbs. First, he can create a certain amount of invisibility for a short period of time. Notice how the weedy Plantain manages to make himself so inconspicuous? That's a power that you can harness, especially if you are doing astral journeying to other worlds.

Second, he can be used in recels (Northern Tradition smudging incense) to speak to the ancestors, or to find your way to the Hel Road. His name "Waybread" echoes this usage - Waybread will help you find the way. If you actually manage to get yourself astrally wounded, Plantain is the plant to resort to. In some cases, he can even save you from astral death, if your body is still healthy. His regenerative gift of bringing flesh back to life doesn't work on the physical plane, but I have good reason to suspect that it works on other planes. Certainly Grandfather Waybread himself has made allusions to this fact. Since I've not ever been astrally killed by enemies, I've never been in a position to experiment. Those who find the need to implement it should let me know how it goes.

Plantain is a very important herbal "drawer", meaning that his main job is to draw out infection. He is used in an ointment, or an external wash, or in an emergency just packing on the chewed leaf, to draw out splinters, foreign objects, insect venom, and even snake venom. For the latter two, the poultice or wash must be done fairly immediately. While he may not get everything out, he can make the difference between living long enough to get to the hospital or not. Plantain draws infection out from all wounds, removing pus and closing the flesh. He is especially good for infections in the teeth and gums, even when abscesses spread to other parts of the head. He is good for dirty wounds when you may not be able to get ground-in dirt out of the flesh, and will treat the nastiest, most horrible oozing infections. Externally, he is used in ointment or wash for wounds, burns, hemorrhoids, sores, boils, inflammations, conjunctivitis, ringworm infestations, Nettle stings, thrush, chicken pox, and shingles.

He is also used internally to help the urinary tract, kidneys, and bladder. Plantain heals gastrointestinal ulcers and is used to get out deep-seated bronchial infection. He will repair lungs damaged by breathing in harmful materials, removing the particles and expelling them. (Expect to cough up a lot of pus, though.) Plantain is a confirmed antimicrobial that stimulates healing processes. He has been used to help stop smoking, as he makes tobacco smoke taste bad, and cleanse the lungs out afterwards.

Uniquely among many herbs, Plantain can be either astringently drying or moistening depending on the needs of the situation. This means that you don't need to worry about diagnosing a wet or dry condition incorrectly – Grandfather Plantain will simply assess the situation and do whichever action is more appropriate. His action is cooling – this is a very earthy plant, close to the Earth and reflecting that – and nourishing.

The acupuncture point that is associated with Plantain – the "door" through which this plant spirit travels most easily – is Kidney 15. Press gently on that point after ingesting him or using his leaves as a poultice.

The seeds are used as bird and poultry feed, and were ground for flour by hungry travelers; thus its name Waybread. Their mucilage is high in fiber and lowers cholesterol. My naturopath recommended using the ground seeds of Waybread in bread and cookie recipes to cut down my cholesterol.

For a medicinal Plantain charm that anyone can make, even if you live in the city: Gather about a pound of fresh Plantain leaves and put them through the food processor until they're a paste – not an easy thing, as Plantain is full of stringy fibers which may need to be fished out. Once you have green paste, blend with a cup of olive oil. Then heat it gently on the stove and slowly grate in beeswax using a fine grater. You know you've put in enough when you can dip in a spoon. Let it cool and the stuff firms up and becomes salve-like but not candle-hard. Keep it refrigerated unless you're traveling with it, and when you rub it on, you can either sing or recite the Waybread verse of the Nine Herbs Song (if you happen to know it), or say the charm below. Grandfather Waybread will help to regenerate the flesh quicker.

Snakeweed, slay the serpent's bite,
Ripple Grass, rip the grief from my flesh,
Waybread, bear the invader away.

He smiles at me from under his slouch hat, from beneath his tattered moustache. A gnarled staff swings in his hand. "You walked that road," he says, and I realize suddenly that he is talking about my near-death experience, many years ago. "I saw you there, but you didn't get far." He scans the horizon. "Good thing, that. Would have missed you, Being as I knew we'd come to know each other someday."

"Do you know what road I'll be walking next?" I hold my breath, but he squints and just smiles.

"Can't say. But I'll walk with you, even if you don't see me. Isn't the walking of it the point?"

Rosemary for Remembrance

By Alaric Albertsson

he is native to the Mediterranean, and has the inexplicable allure so often found in ladies from that part of the world. Her scent is at once intriguing and stimulating. Because of her charms, men have carried her to the far corners of the Earth. She is attractive and sensuous, a comfort and an ally, and her name is Rosemary.

If you require a more formal introduction, allow me to introduce you to Rosmarinus officinalis. Her name means "dew of the sea" because, in her native lands, she often derives most of the moisture she needs from the sea breeze. It is said that when the goddess Aphrodite arose from the sea, she was draped with this aromatic herb. Rosemary quickly won the hearts of men and the respect of philosopher scientists in both Greece and Rome. Pliny, Dioscorides, and Galen all wrote about this useful herb. From the earliest times, Rosemary ingratiated herself in every arena of the human experience: flavoring our food and drink, enhancing our beauty, perfuming our homes, and relieving our discomfort. Few herbs have brought so much into our lives. But Rosemary was too independent to remain on the Mediterranean coast. Europeans carried her northward to England and the Netherlands, and from there her journey continued around the world.

A member of the mint family, Rosemary has a delightful fragrance evoking images of virgin pine forests. This fragrance is strongest in the herb's needle-like evergreen leaves. The flowers in mature specimens are usually blue, although cultivars have been developed with white, pink, or violet blossoms. Under ideal growing conditions Rosemary can reach a height of five feet or more.

Rosemary stimulates and nurtures what the Anglo-Saxons called the *myne*, the part of you that embodies both your emotions and your memories. For this reason she became an herb with both amorous and funereal associations. Young lovers once exchanged bouquets including a few sprigs of Rosemary "for remembrance". Brides wore or carried rosemary wreaths tied with ribbon. This same property – remembrance – is why rosemary was also used in funeral wreaths.

With her reputation for being an energizing herb, Rosemary has long been appreciated for her protective, healing qualities. Rosemary was once burned in sickrooms to cleanse the air. In the 16th century the herbalist John Gerard asserted that this plant "comforts the heart and makes it merry." Seventy years later, Rosemary was carried to ward off the plague.

Rosemary's value as a remedial herb is especially efficacious for cold conditions. Brew an infusion (tea) of the leaves to help relieve colds, influenza, and rheumatic pains. The infusion can also help people suffering from insomnia.

Rosemary wine can be a good tonic for the nerves. This is a simple cold infusion that anyone can make. Chop up fresh rosemary leaves until you have two full tablespoons. Put this in a jar or bottle and cover it with a fifth of white wine. Store the mixture for two days in a cool dark place, then strain out the solid bits. Sip a small glass of infused wine as needed.

This herb is also good for the scalp and hair. An infusion of the leaves, cooled down, can be used as a hair rinse to reduce dandruff. Or dilute a few drops of the essential oil in a tablespoon of cold pressed almond oil, and use this for massaging the scalp to help stimulate hair growth.

Rosemary shampoo can be used daily for an ongoing treatment of the scalp and hair. To make this you will need several branches of the fresh herb, four drops of Rosemary essential oil, five ounces of unscented baby shampoo, and a cup of distilled water. Strip the leaves off the branches. Simmer the leaves in the distilled water uncovered, for about thirty minutes. By this time, the liquid should be reduced to half.

Strain this decoction and let the water cool. Add the shampoo and essential oil to the water and mix these together well.

As a spiritual herb, Rosemary has found a place in many religions. Sprigs of the herb have been found in Egyptian tombs. Rosemary was burned at temple altars in ancient Greece. As she moved northward, the Germanic people readily accepted her into their culture. In the Netherlands she was called "elf leaf", and was believed to be favored by the elves (nature spirits). Rosemary is even found in Christian folklore. According to legend, the blossoms of this herb were originally white until the Virgin Mary draped her cloak over a bush, turning the flowers blue. (Apparently the dye in the cloak was not colorfast.)

Rosemary, as an herb that stimulates the memory, can be useful in any love spell because, of course, you want that special someone to remember you. A love poppet can be constructed for this purpose. The goal is to implant yourself in the other person's myne; you aren't setting a snare for a hapless victim. It is important that the other person is available and at least marginally interested in you. To make a love poppet, cut two identical human shapes – with head, torso, arms, and legs from cotton or linen cloth to construct a doll roughly nine to twelve inches in height. On the front piece, stitch the name of your special someone across the chest area in red thread. Keep the image of this person vivid in your mind's eye as you sew. Try to recall the person's odor and the sound of their voice. If you wish, facial features can be stitched onto the head, using whatever color thread appeals to you.

Sew the front and back halves of the body together, leaving an opening at the top of the head. Fill the poppet with Rosemary leaves at any time between sunset on Thursday and sunset on Friday. This is the evening and the day sacred to the goddess Frigga, who governs marriages. The fresh leaves are easier to work with while doing this. If you must use dried leaves, break them up to prevent the needles from catching in the cloth. After filling the poppet, stitch the opening shut. Keep the love poppet with you as much as you can. Sleep with it under your bed or pillow. When it has fulfilled its function, the poppet may be burned in the hearth or on an outdoor fire.

Rosemary is described as a tender perennial, which means this hot-blooded lady will freeze to death if the temperature drops below 30 degrees Fahrenheit. In climates similar to her native Mediterranean home, Rosemary can thrive all through the year. Once when I was in San Francisco, I noticed the familiar needle-like leaves on a hedge that ran the entire length of a city block. Pinching off the tip of a branch, I sniffed the leaves and recognized Rosemary's woodsy scent. I have also seen healthy bushes standing four to five feet in height in English gardens. In much of the United States, however, this herb must be brought inside before the first frost hits.

Some people advise planting Rosemary in the ground in northern climates and then digging her up each fall. I think it is hard on the plant to uproot and pot it, especially since the move indoors will be a shock in itself. In my experience, Rosemary does better if you give her a large pot and leave her in it, bringing the pot inside the house during the winter. The pot should be as large as you can manage, and somewhat porous.

Keep in mind, though, that Rosemary is not a houseplant. She hates being indoors. You can woo her to the best of your ability, but the most you can hope for is tolerance on her part until you can return her to the great outdoors. Ideally she should be kept cool. And ideally she should have a minimum of six to eight hours of sunlight each day. These conditions tend to be mutually exclusive; therefore some compromise usually must be met. I keep mine in the winter next to the sliding door leading to our back patio. There she receives plenty of sunlight, and enjoys an occasional brief cold breeze when someone opens and closes the door.

The thing Rosemary hates the most about indoor living is the lack of humidity. You can't make up for this by watering her more often, and in fact she would rather her soil be kept slightly dry. But Rosemary needs humidity. She should be misted several times a day. For most of us, this is not going to happen, but at the very least she should be misted two or three times each week.

Even so, artificial misting is only a substitute for natural humidity. The best thing you can do for your Rosemary, in a northern climate, is to take her outside on those rare winter days when the temperatures rise into the forties and fifties Fahrenheit. Let her enjoy the fresh air while she can, but be sure to bring her back in before the cold weather returns. This year my Rosemary spent most of New Year's Day out on the back patio where, when she was not looking, I caught her sipping mimosas and exchanging gossip with the holly bush. Rosemary loves being outdoors, and even a few hours will revive her spirits if you have a warm afternoon in February when she can get out of the house.

Harvesting Rosemary

For cooking, spell work, incense, or any other purpose – it's quite simple. Just cut the ends of the branches off. Since she is a perennial, take no more than a third of the length of a branch. This does not hurt the plant; it encourages growth. The leaves are then easily stripped from the branch.

New Rosemary plants can be propagated from the ends of the branches. When the moon is waxing (growing from new to full) snip off a two inch sprig from a mature plant and strip the leaves from the lower half. Dip this part in rooting hormone, available at any garden center, and then plant the dipped end in a seed starting mix of peat moss and vermiculite. Let the moon complete one full cycle, and by this time the cutting should have new roots. Once she is well established, pinch off the tip so she will branch out. Give her plenty of sun, good drainage, and remember to bring her indoors each fall if you live in a northern climate. Treat her well, and Rosemary may stay with you for twenty years or more.

Sources

Beyerl, Paul. *The Master Book of Herbalism.* Custer, WA: Phoenix Publishing, 1984.

Bremness, Lesley. *The Complete Book of Herbs.* New York: Viking Studio Books, 1988.

Hemphill, Rosemary. *Herbs for all Seasons.* New York: Viking Penguin, 1993.

Ody, Penelope. *The Complete Medicinal Herbal.* New York: Dorling Kindersley, 1993.

Rose, Jeanne. *Herbs & Things.* New York: Grosset & Dunlap, 1972.

Schneebeli-Morrell, Deborah. *The Victorian Book of Potions and Perfumes.* Godalming, Surrey: S. Webb & Son, 1995.

Rosemary and Wood Betony: Protectress and Prankster

By Ann Moura

wo of my favorite plants are rosemary and wood betony. Both have a variety of benefits in the magical, culinary, and physical realms, and both are very easy to grow. Rosemary grows into a shrubby pine-like bush and does not mind having its tips trimmed for magical, culinary, and medicinal purposes, but it is not fond of deep trimming and abhors heavy pruning. Wood betony is a carefree weed that thrives anywhere and puts on a happy face in the garden while quietly plotting to take over the domain.

I live in central Florida, and here I have maintained a rosemary plant for as long as 15 years, until a terrible frost did it in while I was away. That same year a new rosemary plant begged me to rescue it from a home improvement store's garden section where it was doomed for the dumpster if it didn't sell that week. Marked down outrageously and stuck on a shelf with withered and dying plants, it was a pitiful sight indeed. Yes, plants talk. You can hear them if you just listen. Of course it is best if either of you have something to say to avoid the "first date" syndrome of awkward silence. In this case it was quite loud and clear. Plants know when you can hear them, and this little rosemary cried out, "SAVE ME!" -- so I did.

I brought it home, and speaking soothingly to it, I planted it in the same spot where the deceased rosemary had been. The new plant knew at once the jobs ahead for it, for rosemary is a plant with a strong magical energy of protection and purification, as well as attraction for the Fair Folk. Being planted by the door of the house, rosemary shows that the dwellers are receptive to Faerie visits, and this was further emphasized by the large number of elder trees in the yard, all of which are the transplanted from the offshoots of one elder rescued from a construction site. Rosemary is also a plant of love and fidelity, often used in floral wedding arrangements and for Yuletide wreaths. The aroma of rosemary is cleansing and purifying, and a few sprigs make a fine addition to any balefire. At the head of the herb garden, next to the back door, the little rosemary grew quickly into a nice size shrub.

Wood betony (or just plain betony), on the other hand, is a mischievous imp of a plant. It has the magical energy of protection and purification, but also that of psychic awareness and the ability to bring peace of mind. It likes to giggle when it thinks it has gotten away with something. In my case, it settled into the herb garden like a dutiful little plant with a twinkle of knowing in its floral eye. Within a short time, I was discovering betony all over the garden! Carefully pulling up one plant revealed the hidden truth about betony -- it profusely spreads by root. I spent most of that season pulling up betony and setting it in the bare spots of the yard to grow with abandon. Every once in a while, while working in the herb garden I would hear a giggle. I would look around the foliage of the herbs and discover a little betony laughing at the prank of invading the garden. They never mind being gently removed, their long white root tendrils being eased out of the soil, and are almost cuddly when being placed out in the yard where they have quickly become ground cover for the bare patches.

Rosemary likes the sun, air circulation, and a sandy soil that has good drainage -- you don't want to crowd it. In central Florida, the sun is quite intense, so I prefer to use the north side of the house for the herb garden. Although there is lots of sunlight, there is also a bit of protection. Because the area is mainly free of frost, rosemary grows year round. When a frost is threatened, I carefully cover the plants with old bed sheets. If the temperature in your area drops below 30 degrees Fahrenheit, it is better to keep rosemary in a container that you can bring indoors during the cold weather, just be sure to keep it where there is plenty of sunlight. Make sure also that the pot allows for good drainage, such as with terra cotta ones.

With humidity and lack of breeze, rosemary can develop a white powdery mildew, so be sure to keep the soil drained, give it at least 6 hours of sunlight (or artificial light), and place it where there is a breeze, even if only that of a fan. If your rosemary is in a container, the soil of the pot will need to be replaced yearly.

If it outgrows the pot, transfer it to a larger pot. Another option is to trim the sides and bottom of the roots and replant in the same pot, but trim a little off the top of the shrub as well. The plant will take a deep breath and start to regrow.

Rosemary can be an ornamental plant in the garden or around the house and yard, but it also has a lovely fragrance and can be used in cooking. Leaves and flowers are both edible, and you can snip off a piece of stem to add to chicken and savory dishes. It is also a good additive to tea for aiding digestion as it relaxes the stomach, although too much rosemary can irritate the stomach, the digestive tract, and kidneys, so as with all things, moderation is best. It is good for relieving a headache, aiding the circulation, or as a general tonic. Rosemary is said to help prevent liver toxicity, and have anticancer and antitumor properties. A tea makes a good expectorant when flu or colds strike, and it is good for coughs and relieving stress.

Rosemary oil soothes muscle aches, sores, and minor skin injuries such as bruises and scrapes. A few rosemary sprigs in olive oil will flavor the oil for cooking, but remove the sprigs after two or three weeks to avoid deterioration. Rosemary is used to flavor wine, baked in bread, and added to shampoo to stimulate hair growth.

Wood betony prefers woodlands and shady places, but it will also grow in open meadows, and in the garden it will find its own shade under larger herbs if given a chance. There it will hide and send out its tendrils beneath the soil to conquer the garden. It is happy in full sun or partial shade, being versatile and adaptive to its environment.

The Latin name of the European Wood Betony is Stachys officinalis, and should not to be confused with Pedicularis (Lousewort). As a protective plant, it has been used for centuries to ward negative magic and malice. As a medicinal plant, it is said to stimulate the heart and is good for cardiovascular disorders. Wood betony also eases hyperactivity and aids against chronic headache, probably through its sedative properties. When treating colds, tension headache, or migraines, the herb may be used fresh, dried, in tea, or made into a tincture. Wood betony is also good for relieving stress and nervous tension, and can be combined with a little comfrey and linden (tila) flower for sinus headache and nasal congestion. As a tea, pour a cup of boiling water over 1 to 2 teaspoons of the dried herb (leaves and/or flowers).

Magical uses for rosemary and betony are many. Add rosemary to a yellow candle for good health or to a blue one for healing. Use rosemary oil to anoint a yellow candle for mental clarity and improved memory or anoint a gold, green, or orange candle for success, growth, or gains in business or legal matters.

Add rosemary to a black candle for protection, or to a red candle for energy and vigor. Add rosemary to a pink candle for happiness or anoint a white candle with rosemary oil for blessing. Combine rosemary in a charm bag with betony and place in an area for cleansing and clearing away negative energy.

Add betony to a white candle for cleansing a space; or to a black candle for protection. Blend with fennel, marjoram, rosemary, and woodruff in a charm bag for protection and place in a car. Add betony to a purple candle for psychic enhancement or to a lavender candle for Faerie communication.

As with all magic, ask a plant to help you with your needs and wait a moment to see what portion seems brighter or more apparent as an offered portion. Wait until you sense that the spirit of the plant has withdrawn from the portion offered. Give a gift to receive a gift, be it water for the plant, crushed eggshells, a blessing, or other such gift before cutting a piece for your use. To use in magic, lift the portion over your altar and call upon the plant's magical power with your intent, set it on the pentacle, and hold your palms over the herb and consecrate it to your use through the Elementals and the Goddess and the God.

If the plant offers nothing to you, the meaning may be that it feels you should be addressing a different plant or the intent is not appropriate for it. I have had a Mugwort plant scream "NO!" to me when I sought to trim it for a wreath, then it explained that it would die if trimmed at that time, so I left it alone and used instead a jasmine plant who offered me tendrils for a wreath. A few weeks later I heard a "YooHoo!" in the garden and I saw the Mugwort large and bushy, offering me a portion for a wreath. In magic, one never refuses a gift, so I made another wreath, this time to honor the plants of the garden and protect them from harm. The point here is that if a plant is not willing to work with you, there is a reason. Check the health and condition of the plant and see what you can do to help if needed. Otherwise, rethink your use for the plant and consider whether or not there is another herb you should be using, or your purpose needs better defining or direction. The plants understand on an empathic level – perhaps the one that is unwilling to help has sensed something in you that needs clarification or better planning. They understand that in magic especially, we must adhere to the rule of "Harm None" and they will often offer guidance by holding back their energy until we are on the right track, or we need to utilize a different herb altogether.

Rosemary and wood betony are two versatile and enthusiastic plants, eager to help anyone who takes the time to call upon them. Plant a rosemary shrub by your door to protect your home, and plant wood betony in a container to keep the roots from wandering. Thin the wood betony as needed, perhaps releasing into a barren area that needs ground cover, or harvesting for magical or herbal use. Listen for the cheery giggle of wood betony, offering brightness and joy in your surroundings. Feel the gentle protective energy of rosemary, alert and on duty guarding your home. Remember that we are all connected through Spirit, and we are all One.

Vervain

By Kurt Hunter

ervain, or Verbena, is a genus in the family
Verbenaceae containing approximately 250 species of
annual and perennial flowering plants. Most have
been introduced from Canada or Europe to other
parts of the world. The leaves are often small and medium to
dark green, being hairy or dusty in appearance. The flowers are
pink, white, magenta, or purple with five petals and born in
dense clusters. The plants themselves are drought resistant and
prefer rocky or upturned soil with good drainage and tolerate
full to partial sun. Once grown from seed, they require little
care and will spread out quickly.

Vervain is considered a weed by most today but has a long
and respected history throughout human civilization. In
Ancient Egypt it was called "Tears of Isis" and later on in
Roman culture it was known as "Tears of Juno". Pliny the Elder
describes the plant being presented at the altars of Jupiter for
blessings of abundance and success. It was also placed on altars
of Venus and Diana, giving rise to the theory that the word
Verbena was merely a "catch-all" to suggest any kind of
sacrificial plant offering. Christian folklore stated that Vervain
was used to staunch Jesus' wounds after he was removed from
the cross. Afterward it became known simply as "Holy Herb".
In Wales it was called "Devil's Bane" due to its protective
characteristics. Other names include Dragon's Claw,
Enchanter's Plant, Demetria, Moradilla, Pigeon's Grass, Herba
Veneris (herb of Venus), Herba Sacra (sacred herb), and Herb of
Grace, amongst others. In modern magickal lore the plant is
viewed as feminine and sacred to Venus and the element of
earth (though some would say water).

Pictures of the flowers can be found on many magickal
engravings including anti-Stregheria charms and in the

preparation of a Mandragora charm. William Hazlitt in his Dictionary of Faiths and Folklore (1905) quotes John Aubrey's Miscellanies (1696) saying "Vervain and Dill / Hinder Witches from their Will". The Druids included it in their lustral (holy) water where it was gathered under the dark of the moon with the star Sirius in the heavens, though practically it can be gathered at any time so long as it is flowering or just before. The water was used for divination and the purification of sacred places. Vervain was also likely employed by magicians to purify themselves before their rites as well as being commonly used by cunning folk for their potions and healing charms over the centuries. In the British Isles, people held the herb over the Beltane fire to protect their livestock and strewed it over the fields at Summer Solstice to ensure fertility.

Vervain's strong protective qualities also come from stories of Roman soldiers carrying springs of it with them into battle, and homes being sprinkled with an infusion of it to ward off evil. Drinking the tea is said to help in astral work and the opening of the inner eye, so for this reason some give the plant's astrological association as Mercury rather than Venus.

Today it has several uses in the practice of Witchcraft. It is commonly used in magickal purification baths. Burn solitary Vervain, or with equal parts of Frankincense, for a fantastic purification incense. It can be used to make amulets of protection and to attract wealth. The dried herb sprinkled about the home attracts prosperity as well as peace and contentment. Hung from the bed it drives away nightmares. Plant Vervain in the garden or as a houseplant to attract money and improve the health of other plants. Worn on the person, it allows escape from one's enemies and can be of aid in the preparation of charms of invisibility or shapeshifting. It is also used in many love sachets, especially to ensure fidelity and chastity. One legend states that if you gather Vervain before sunrise on the New Moon, press out its juice, and drink it down, you will lose all desire for sex for seven years. For many, this may be too extreme a solution for calming sexual urges but it reinforces the notion of the power the herb has over sex. One could also burn Vervain to dispel an unrequited love, in oneself or another. Rather than being an herb that attracts love, it is one that repels energies that are disharmonious to creating or maintaining a loving relationship. It decreases anxiety and improves our ability to navigate through the sometimes treacherous waters of romance. It has also been observed that burning it can aid one in contacting the dead, though this is probably again as part of a purification rite to make the space easier for such efforts to take place. Ultimately, Vervain is one of the few herbs that can be used without disharmonious effect in almost any magickal situation. It has the effect of negating energies that are at cross-purpose with the Witch's intention.

Medicinally, infusions of Vervain are used to treat insomnia, stress and nervous tension, and promote an overall sense of well-being. It relaxes tension so individuals who feel edgy or fragmented can experience healing and wholeness. It is used as a liver stimulant to improve poor appetite and digestion, and as an expectorant and diuretic. A tincture of Vervain can be used to treat kidney stones. A poultice is helpful for sprains, bruises, and insect bites. Ointments are applied to eczema, wounds, and weeping sores. Vervain tea is a common, relaxing drink in many parts of the world. It has effects both as a tonic and as a sedative, and some serve it for its properties as an aphrodisiac. Care should be used in its application. Most people find it mildly calming, but for a few, the effects can be more sedating.

My own experiences with Vervain include: as a vital ingredient to love potions or sachets, especially when one's intention is on commitment and faithfulness. It also helps in avoiding the missteps that can be all too common with dating today. Bathing with a few drops of Vervain elixir added to your bath creates a peaceful yet invigorating soak with the end result of appearing and feeling more youthful and calm, ready to absorb whatever lessons the Universe is showing at the time, whether they be about loving oneself or another. It is wonderful to sprinkle or anoint oneself with Vervain water prior to astral journeys as it makes them more clear and profound. Tea with Vervain, Chamomile and Peppermint is a great way to wind down the day before bedtime. The Spirit of Vervain takes well to working with others in the Green Kingdom and, in fact, is very difficult to use improperly in most situations. The plant has a gentle yet constant protective and balancing quality and wants to cooperate with the Witch.

The following is an easy example of one of Vervain's many uses.

Happy Home Powder

2 parts Vervain
2 parts Thyme
1 part Basil
1 part Lavender

Sprinkle about, either the outside of the home (to prevent disharmonious elements from entering) or a tiny bit at the baseboards in each of the rooms to preserve happy energies within. This powder has a very benign energy. Combined with 2 parts of Benzoin or Frankincense as loose incense,it can be burned on a charcoal which does wonders in clearing and setting the space for happiness and prosperity to enter. As an added bonus, this is also an excellent blend for promoting restful sleep and banishing nightmares.

Yarrow

Or, Why A Little Warrior Spirit is a Good Thing, Even for Non-Violent Types

By Grayforest

 ost of my experiences with plants has not been in the context of magickal ritual, but more in the context of cooking and healing. Thus went my initial encounter with yarrow, also known as Achillea millefolium. It was not a formal ritual use, but in retrospect, it was a fine example of "magick in action".

In my first quarter of botanical medicine as a naturopathic medical student, I was asked to simply get to "know" a plant by spending time with it daily. This would balance out the more left-brained work of memorizing names and constituents and dosages and help us learn the energetic signature of the plant. For as healers know, plants are much more than a stew of biochemistries and cellulose. They are healing entities in themselves.

So originally I thought I would try the Elliot Cowan Plant Spirit approach (which emphasizes getting to know plants as indigenous healers do). I would meditate with my plant, draw it, sit quietly with it, and imbibe its lessons.

But first I had to choose a plant, preferably one nearby where I lived, as this approach requires that I actually be in said plant's presence on a daily basis. The choosing kept getting shoved aside as the quarter went by, with all the unexpected things that I'd learned to expect. Life moved faster, somehow, than life seemed to have a right to move. A hospitalized parent and corollary sibling issue, meetings regarding a child's slow progress in school, teens testing their new growth — the many needs and wants of family seemed louder than usual, even for our normally busy household. My partner, who had been seeing too much of the household needs during my first two years in my degree program, found his workload soaring with new responsibilities and additional hours.

The household task tending teetered back towards my end. He needed to work; I had school; we both have kids who needed us. I found myself yearning to set boundaries that honored all parties — myself included. Especially since I needed to go spend time, daily, with an herb.

Enter my yarrow.

Ever since I heard Eric Yarnell, N.D. quoted as having called Yarrow "the gateway to Western medicine", I had been curious about yarrow. In my pre-Bastyr years of using herbs, yarrow wasn't one of the ones that tended to get much attention on the store shelves and in the press. How was it the "gateway to modern medicine"? So the year prior to my assignment, I had set out to make its acquaintance. Serendipitously finding a yarrow plant at a rural nursery, I set it in a former water fountain in our front yard, now gone condo into an herb bed. I am not known for raising plants successfully, but unexpectedly, the herb bed thrived, and the yarrow in it. Perhaps that was no surprise. Yarrow thrives many places, from weedy city lots (at least in the Pacific Northwest) to high mountain ranges across the West. In gravel bars, clearings, roadsides — it can be dry or moist, but yarrow likes it open. It's not one for skulking in the shadows.

The yarrow turned out to be of an oddish variety — bearing flat-topped clusters of tiny, composite yellow flowers instead of white, and there was discussion as to what impact this might have on its constituents. While Achillea species are often used interchangeably, it does turn out that there are chromosomal differences among them, and thus differences in the amount of medicinal constituents. The bed was shallow, and thus the fern-like, finely feathery leaves, "pinnately dissected", and then dissected again, never did reach the full 100 cm height that yarrow aspires to. But it took deep rhizomatous root among the sage and curry, overwhelming the oregano, fending off the lemon balm, standing its ground against an egotistical (but lovable) chamomile that claimed all the territory within the circle of its leaf tips.

The late herbalist Michael Moore (not the film one), claims yarrow to be good for colds and flu (Moore, 1993). Even before the flowers bloomed, I took a few leaves from its adolescent growth to brew into a tea to fend off a summer virus spreading through my household. At that time I thought it was mainly the flowers that were used; but the leaves seemed to stop whatever was in its tracks, just the same. Perhaps I was already listening to the plant, as later I found that the young, small leaves do indeed have a long history of use. I found the taste not unpleasant, sort of light and perhaps not memorable. Something I could drink without much thought, neither grimacing as it went down nor craving it for sweetness.

The yarrow grew. Bees loved it. We picked flower heads, periodically, using kitchen scissors to snip off the tough stems. We stashed them away, with more enthusiasm than knowledge; how was I to know that the ubiquitous kitchen moth would feast on yarrow, as well? Mid-winter I discovered wings and eggs among my plastic bagged flower heads. I was left with the commercial loose tea and a tincture, which I took at times to deal with various inflammations and conditions. However, I tended to forget it next to the tulsi and lemon ginger.

All this occurred the summer and winter prior to the class assignment. When it came time to do an herbal monograph — well, I thought, I had best find something new to study. That decision kept getting pushed back amidst the meetings and phone calls and my partner's 3 a.m. on-call workloads.

And then, one wet, delayed spring day, with a moment to check the outside beds, I discovered that the yarrow, a perennial, had come back. It was already nearly as big as its full growth the prior year, waving new fern-like leaves next to a lavender in exuberant growth. I looked around at the old roses, the Geranium robertum, the hydrangeas, sparse tulips, and wet withered stems of last year's plantings. I looked back at the yarrow, which had that odd shy self-confidence of any young teenager, all modest brashness. Did I remember at that moment, what had been commented in class about yarrow and one's need to perhaps put a little warrior into one's life? In its best sense, what is that code-speak for but to "draw a boundary: this far and no further?" I did not remember that consciously; but at that moment I took it on.

Yarrow's very name, *Achillea millefolium,* reflects its long association with warriors and wounds, and it has been used for that by purpose by both Greeks and Cherokee, European, and Native American. Achilles was a Greek mythological hero who was supposed to have been rendered immortal by being dipped in the river Styx. Yarrow's long list of traditional uses sound as if it could very nearly render one, if not immortal, then at least well-defended against what may come during a long and busy life. And in many of these uses we can see where it performs the function of a "healthy warrior": helping to maintain boundaries.

Dioscorides described using pounded yarrow leaves as a vulnerary on fresh wounds to help speed closure and healing: helping the body close a breach in its most obvious boundary, the skin. Native Americans also applied the chewed leaves to burns, bruises, sores, sprains, swellings, and wounds. Astringent, hemostatic, anti-inflammatory, yarrow sets physical, mucosal boundaries: it stops bleeding, pushes back inflammation, astringent and hemostatic. Both bleeding and inflammation are good things in their time and place, necessary responses to breach and invasion, but so far, no further needs to be said at one point. And it is one thing we can remember as we deal with the wounds in our own lives: often it's the case that what is now causing harm is not, in and of itself, "bad". It is more a matter of degree and balance and timing.

Antipyretic, it is used in acute fevers (especially those of colds and flu), inducing a sweat — which among other things, helps the body discharge unhealthy substances ranging from nicotine to mercury. Fever can be healing (and a great boundary setting itself); it can also get out of hand. Here again yarrow restores proper boundaries.

Yarrow stalks were thrown by the Chinese in the ancient *I-Ching*, casting and dividing the aspects of situations to sense the flow of energy, delineating the present so that the questioner could assess where to say yes and where to say no: boundaries again. And European folklore states that planting yarrow will bind a couple together. Any close relationship requires boundaries as well as intimacy. Marking out those boundaries can do much to strengthen close relationships, between friends and family members, as well as partners.

As part of the "herbal experience" class assignment, I had been asked to select and take a bitters formula, classically given to assist digestion. Our professor, however, had a further purpose: she wanted us to experience how a particular bitters formulation could change us on a whole-person level. The bitters I chose had yarrow in it, and so even before I said yes to the herb for the class assignment, I experienced its subtle strengthening effects. I began to digest what was happening to me (yarrow was also classically seen as an herb for the digestive tract). I started to sort out what was going on, keeping what I needed to deal with and discarding what did not require my attention. I began to say no where I needed to say no. Experiencing yarrow, it turned out, did not call for sitting or drawing. It needed action "on the ground" in my daily life.

That's magick.

So as I reflect on it, it's interesting that what initially appeared to be a case of "behind on an assignment" turned out, in a way, to be the assignment. For times when the obstacle is the path... look to yarrow.

Sources

Cunningham, S. (2000). *Encyclopedia of Magical Herbs.* Minnesota: Llewellyn Publications.

Foster, S., & Hobbs, C. (2002). *Western Medicinal Plants and Herbs* (Peterson Field Guides). New York, New York: Houghton Mifflin.

Garrett, J. (2003). *The Cherokee Herbal.* Rochester, Vermont: Bear & Company.

Hoffman, D. (2003). *Medical Herbalism.* Rochester, Vermont: Healing Arts Press.

Moore, M. (1993). *Medicinal Plants of the Pacific West.* Santa Fe, New Mexico: Red Crane Books.

Pojar, J., & McKinnon, A. (1994). *Plants of the Pacific Northwest Coast Revised.* Vancouver, BC, Canada: Lone Pine Publishing.

Tierra, M. (1998). *The Way of Herbs.* New York, New York: Pocket Books.

Tilgner, N. S. (1999). *Herbal Medicine From the Heart of the Earth.* Creswell, Oregon: Wise Acres Publishing.

Part Two: The Banes

Belladonna: Walking with the Beautiful Lady

By Matthew Venus

hen one thinks of the classical plants associated with witchcraft, Deadly Nightshade (Atropa Belladonna) is rarely excluded from the list of usual suspects. As many of her common names attest, she is one of the more baneful plants in the witches' apothecary. The deadly poisonous nature of Belladonna and her associations with witchcraft have earned her such monikers as Banewort, Witch's Berry, Sorcerer's Cherry, and Beautiful Death.

It is commonly believed that the name Atropa found its origins in relation to one of the three Greek Moirae, goddesses of fate and destiny. Atropos, the inevitable one, was the Moirae responsible for the timing, and mechanism of each person's death. It was she who ultimately cut the threads of life with her abhorred shears. Through the plants associations with death and the dead, Belladonna is generally attributed to the planetary power of Saturn, though she is sometimes seen as a possessing Martial attributes as well.

The alkaloid Atropine is primarily responsible for gifting Belladonna her poison. In quantity, the toxins in Belladonna can cause dilation of pupils, headaches, tachycardia, loss of coordination, hallucinations, convulsions, paralysis, coma, and eventually death. Many of the same alkaloids found in Belladonna are mirrored in her bewitching cousins, other members of the Solanaceae family such as Datura and Mandrake. It is this commonality which made such plants regular additions to the famed unguentum sabbati, or flying ointment, often associated with witchcraft from the middle ages onward.

The unguentum sabbati was said to assist witches in either the astral flight which lead them to the Sabbat. The common effects reported from use of flying ointments are the feeling of leaving the body, entering heavy trance states, and intense hallucinations. It is said by those who have experienced the hallucinogenic effects of Belladonna that the visions they endure are extremely realistic, have a tendency to feature the dead, and are quite often terrifying. Though I would never suggest that anyone attempt to use Belladonna, either applied topically or ingested for spiritual or recreational purposes, one has to wonder if the terrifying visions offered up by the Genius of Belladonna are the product of her design, or of the mind which informs them.

Due to her highly toxic nature, Belladonna has often found use as a poison. From the accidental poisoning of the troops of Marcus Antonius to her intentional use in dispatching the Danes, there are many historical accounts of Belladonna taking men to their deaths. Though all parts of the plant are poisonous, in cases where she finds her use in intentional poisonings or in the unguentum sabbati, the highly toxic roots and berries of Belladonna are most commonly utilized.

The shiny, succulent, and sweet berries of Belladonna are an unfortunate enticement for the unattended child or unaware adult. In fact, most recorded cases of poisoning by Belladonna occur by the accidental ingestion of her berries, and it is believed that as few as two to three berries may be sufficient to kill a child. The berries of Belladonna are beautifully plump and black. There alluring appearance invites attention and resembles both a tiny blacked scrying sphere, and the dilated pupils the plant is often associated with.

It is believed that the name Belladonna which means "Beautiful Lady" was a reference to the use of the plant in cosmetics and as eye drops which were utilized to give women the "doe eyed" look of dilated pupils. On the surface this may

Belladonna

seem an odd choice of cosmetic aesthetic, however, the dilation of pupils is often an indication of arousal. This is also an indication to others of sexual receptivity which, in turn may cause attraction in response.

Another possible source for Belladonna's name is her association with the Warrior Goddess Bellona whose priests, the *Bellonarii*, were reported to have drank the plant's juice as a part of ritual practices. It is also believed that Roman soldiers would ingest a concoction of Belladonna to inspire fury and frenzy before battle. It is through the plant's associations with Bellona and that Goddess's connection to the Roman God Mars, that Belladonna may be said to fall under the planetary rulership of Mars as well as Saturn.

Belladonna was believed to be a plant which belonged to the Devil himself, particularly in the Kingdom of Bohemia where it was said that he protected the plant night and day. There was one way though, that the would-be wildcrafter might divert the Devil's attentions long enough to harvest the plant. It was said that on Walpurgis Night if a black hen were set loose near the plant, the Devil would be inclined to follow the hen and leave the plant unattended, thus allowing it to be collected. Other tales tell that the plant was left unattended because the Devil had left to attend the Walpurgis Sabbat.

Before one harvests the plant, it is highly recommended that you work with its Genius first and, of course, obtain her permission. In journey work, the Genius of Belladonna often takes the form of a beautiful woman. She is usually envisaged as pale skinned and dark haired with large black pupils. When I have had experiences with her, she has appeared with a small sickle in hand and dressed in a sheer garment of purple, a tone reminiscent of the color of her flowers. For those who may be reluctant to physically harvest baneful plants, bear in mind that there is much that may be learned from interacting with the plant's Genius alone.

The plant itself loves to be sung to and should be sung to of her virtue and beauty when she is harvested. She enjoys the attention of flattering words as well as displays and energy of a sexual nature. Some sources suggest that one should dance naked at midnight, or copulate in front of the plant in order to gain her favor. In addition to all of Belladonna's other attributes, you will most likely find when working with her that she most certainly has a seductive, ensnaring, and sexual component as well.

The action of Belladonna on the physium may be seen as initial indications as to the nature of the plants Genius. The spirit of Belladonna is one of visionary experience and the threshold between the realms of the living and the dead. Parts of the plant, carefully harvested, may be fashioned into appropriate fetishes for works of a necromantic nature where contact with those whom have passed is desired. It is often utilized in works for calling upon the Mighty Dead for assistance in ritual and revelation. For this purpose a small portion of dried leaves may be crushed and added to incense burned in honor of those who have gone before. However, care should be taken when burning the plant and doing so in a well-ventilated space, or preferably outdoors is recommended.

Belladonna's ability to assist in visionary work is another one of her strengths. It is possible to construct a pouch of allied herbs with the dried berries of Belladonna at its heart which, when properly blessed, assists in the reception of spiritual sight.

Additionally the plant may be added to charms to assist in astral flight and crossing the hedge. Along with the attributes previously listed, the root of Belladonna is said to be a powerful fetish similar to Mandrake. In addition to dream and vision work it may also assist in works of love and enchanting, as well as being used as a fetish for good luck in games of chance.

Furthermore, due to Belladonna's Martial energy, the plant may be used in works of powerful protection. It is also an excellent addition to the arsenal during periods of spiritual warfare. In cases when you must go into battle, either literally or figuratively, most will find that when the Genius of the plant is properly wooed, she ensures victory in your endeavors.

For the myriad of virtues that this beautiful and deadly lady offers, Belladonna has enjoyed a long, storied, and infamous history which continues to be expanded upon by magical practitioners today. For those who would come to know her, I offer these words. Meet her at the threshold with sickle in her hand, give her praise, give her love and above all, give her respect. For those who will meet with her, sing to her and find her favor, Belladonna proves to be a most valuable ally.

The Spirit and Magick of Cannabis: The Friend

By Melanie Marquis

ultivated in Asia around 8000 BCE, cannabis has been in the service of man for thousands of years. Providing a sustainable source of food, fuel, fiber, recreational and spiritual intoxication, and medicine, cannabis cultivation had spread throughout Europe, Russia, parts of Africa, and North America by the sixteenth century, and it is still widely, though often illegally, grown around the world. Despite the long history of cannabis use for mundane purposes as well as for magick, the herb has remained largely in the shadows for the last several decades, where it was pushed by the plastics and paper industry-backed marijuana prohibition movement of the 1930's. But as the legal landscape continues to evolve and cannabis use is tolerated in an increasing number of communities, we can once again embrace this sacred plant in the open, reexamining its benefits to humanity, spirituality, and the magickal arts.

The scope of this article is to offer information about the use of cannabis in the context of magick. Though written with the legal cannabis smoker in mind, the ideas presented here can easily be adapted to benefit anyone interested in utilizing the magickal potential of this very wondrous plant. Simply use photos of psychoactive cannabis, or make use of hemp, the legal (though highly regulated) non-psychoactive variety that is widely available in the form of edibles, textiles, papers, oils, and extracts. It won't get you high, but it still packs a magickal punch.

Clearing the Smoke

Marijuana regulation has caused confusion about the difference between industrial hemp and gets-you-stoned pot. Here are the facts. Cannabis is dioecious—meaning that the plants are either male or female, and are unable to self-pollinate. The male plants produce less THC and much more fiber. The female plants produce much more THC and less fiber. Hemp cultivation has developed strains of cannabis that maximize the yield of fiber. This is used to create fuel, cloth, paper, plastics, and more. Smoking any amount of it will not get you high. To produce cannabis that contains a potent amount of high-inducing THC, the female plants are grown in isolation, separated from the males early on so that the bud does not get pollinated and become seedy. Light exposure is then carefully manipulated at the right times and in the right ways, causing the plant to flower and produce the THC-rich buds that many of us love to smoke. For the purposes of this article, the term "hemp" will be used only to refer to non-psychoactive cannabis, whereas "cannabis" will generally refer to the psychoactive, smokable type.

Lord of Matter, Lady of Spirit, Magickal Marijuana

Hemp and THC-rich cannabis each have their own unique uses and correspondences in magick and spirituality. With its gendered varieties and its powerful, mystical, unique specializations, the cannabis plant serves as a botanical metaphor for the God and Goddess and their qualities. The male hemp, with its strong fibers and nutritious seeds, provides the raw material for creation. From the body of the male plant, we make clothing, food, shelter, and more. It is the material, the active principle, the outward manifestation—a symbol of the God, embodying strength, energy, and actualization. In contrast, the female cannabis plant offers more spiritual benefits. Like the Goddess, the female cannabis comforts, guides, and inspires, expanding perceptions and increasing psychic power. It is the spiritual principle, the internal and eternal idea from which all outward manifestations must spring. Analogous to magick itself, the male hemp correlates to the will of the witch, whereas the female cannabis corresponds to the witch's consciousness and intent.

A Kind Spirit

The cannabis plant embodies a spirit of kindness and compassion, understanding and unity. It is very much a helper plant for humankind, providing us not only with a sustainable source of food, fiber, fuel, and medicine, but also offering us a reason to get together in the shared comfort of a joyful experience, promoting peace, friendship, and community. It helps us forge connections with each other, with Nature, with spirit, and even with disconnected parts of our own inner workings. It gives us a sense of community, a sense of friendship. In fact, a Rastafari term for getting higher, "Iya," also means, "friend." The spirit of cannabis is kind, and if we are to get the most out of our workings with the plant, we must be kind, as well—to the plant, to the planet, to ourselves, and to each other. This means never wasting, never over-indulging to the point of gluttony, and it also means sharing—your herb, a kind word, a new perspective. Try to purchase locally-grown herbs when possible, and stay away from so-called "swag" that is typically grown in very ecologically unsound ways.

The Gateway Bud

Cannabis critics have named the plant a "gateway drug," and I couldn't agree more. Cannabis serves as a gateway into greater dimensions of reality and expanded consciousness. Some commonly experienced effects of smoking or otherwise ingesting cannabis include anxiety reduction, euphoria, laughter, distortion of time perception, increased sensitivity to environmental stimuli, and heightened awareness of one's own body—all of which can be very helpful in carrying out magickal processes. The THC in the plant's buds and leaves offers a shortcut into the magickal mindset, inducing a state of heightened awareness, intuition, and creativity. It can help the magick worker to clear their head both before and after ritual. During ritual, it can serve as a gateway into the inner workings of reality, offering a sense of the oneness of the universe and all that is in it.

Gods of the Green

Cannabis has been associated with life and death goddesses, solar gods, and with deities exhibiting a balance of both male and female qualities. Cannabis is often seen as a sacred symbol to such gods and goddesses, woven into religious myths and incorporated into spiritual worship. Deities linked to the cannabis plant include the Hindu deities Kali Ma, a creator/destroyer goddess, Shiva, often called the "Lord of the Bhang," and Parvati, who restored peace and unity when she introduced Shiva to a pungent, flowering plant many believe to be cannabis. In Germany, Freya, who, like Kali Ma, is a goddess of life and death, has also been associated with the cannabis plant. Ashera, a semetic goddess equated to the "Queen of Heaven," and Ba'al, an early semetic solar god, have likewise been linked to the sacred herb. In Shinto, a native religion of Japan, cannabis is associated with the solar goddess Amaterasu, and is used for spirit communication, purification, protection, and banishing rituals. In the Rastafari faith, cannabis is considered a gift from Jah, the god, and it is used ceremoniously to aid in reasoning and prayer. Many Neopagans associate cannabis with the lunar goddess and use the plant spiritually as well as magickally.

Magickal Uses

Magickally, cannabis is just as practical and versatile as many other botanicals. It has a wide range of magickal correspondences that differ according to the plant's gender and strain. The male hemp is a useful addition to spells for strength, courage, defense, energy, action, and tenacity, and it can be used ritualistically to invoke the God. The female cannabis, which can be used to invoke the goddess, is beneficial in spells to encourage psychism, happiness, peace, intuition, inspiration, and creativity, and is also helpful in healing blends, banishing charms, and purification spells. Nonpoisonous and nutritious, the plant can be used in drinkable potions and brews, and can be used in powders and herbal sachets, as well.

Setting up a Cannabis Altar

Creating an altar space dedicated to the spirit of the cannabis plant will help you develop a closer relationship with the plant's spirit and will also make it easier to make use of its magickal properties. Green is of course the obvious color choice for the altar cloth, but you could instead use a beige-colored cloth woven from natural hemp fibers. A splash of gold for the sun and silver for the moon make nice additions to the basic color scheme. You might decorate the altar with images of cannabis' ruling deities, such as Freya, Kali Ma, or Shiva. If it's legal for you to do so, use bits of real cannabis in your altar decor—a leaf, some seeds, a branch from the harvested plant, a small piece of the flowering bud. You might also wish to incorporate symbols of the sun or the moon—the sun, as it is intrinsically linked with all plants and is an important catalyst for THC production, and the moon, as it is a goddess symbol and representative of the intuition, creativity, and psychic insight the herb is believed by many to impart. Having both a sun symbol and a moon symbol on your cannabis altar does well to represent the dual sexuality of the plant, the sun symbolic of the god-associated male hemp, and the moon symbolic of the female and goddess-associated THC-producing varieties.

Cannabis Magick

The following spells are designed for the licensed, legal cannabis user. For those who can't legally possess or use cannabis, these spells can be adapted to, instead, incorporate hemp foods and other legal hemp products which can be purchased at natural foods stores.

Switching Spell

Whether you want to break a stalemate, create or crack an illusion, or manifest a breakthrough, a switching spell can do the trick. A switching spell twists energies and opens the way to new realities, transforming stagnation into action, altering power structures, and turning perceptional patterns inside out and upside down.

Here's a switching spell that makes use of the transformative power of cannabis. You can incorporate this magick into a full ritual, begun by casting the circle around yourself and the herbs and inviting welcomed spirits and other entities to join in the rite. Or, opt for a quicker method and carry out the magick as a quick charm, leaving out any preliminaries and cutting right to the heart of the spell. Charms generally work best for "right here, right now" magick, producing a quick and sudden, yet typically ephemeral, change in the immediate circumstance or surroundings. Spells are, in contrast, built to last, more far-reaching, and more precisely calculated and carried out in order to affect more powerful or more permanent changes. Match the method to the magick.

Break off a small piece of the herb and balance it gently on your cupped palm. Think of the object of your magick, the stagnation you would like to end, the action or change you would like to stir up. Create a mental image to represent the current reality you wish to transform, and then visualize that image flipping over or twisting, reshaping into something new and better. Do this as you carefully rotate the herb in your hand three times, first turning it over twice along its vertical axis and then spinning it once along its horizontal axis. Pack the herb into a pipe or bong and smoke it while envisioning the desired changes as manifest.

Unifying Spell

Here's a spell to promote unity, peace, and understanding among your immediate circle or in the world at large. Take a rolling paper and hold it with both hands as you conjure a feeling of love and compassion, letting it fill your heart. Envision the people or factions you wish to unify getting along peacefully, perhaps imagining them laughing, shaking hands, or even embracing. As you break apart the cannabis, try to sense the peaceful, compassionate energy in the herb and concentrate on drawing it out and magnifying it, empowering the cannabis to activate its magickal potential. Try to get the herb into an even consistency, removing any seeds or stems. If other people are joining you in your spell, pass around the rolling paper and have each person touch it while thinking of friendship, love, or whatever else the specific goal of the unifying magick might be. Fill the paper with the herb and roll it up, starting from the middle and working out toward the edges. As you seal the rolling paper, state your intent in positive terms, such as, "Our friendship grows and we are united in mind and spirit. We are above petty arguments." Smoke and enjoy.

Goddess Sight Ritual

Try this method of goddess invocation to give psychic awareness a mega-boost. If you have the luxury of legally owning a live cannabis plant, perform your ritual beside it. If not, obtain a photo of a nice-looking cannabis plant and place it on your altar. Look carefully at the growing plant; notice its beauty and intricacy. Try to sense the plant's spirit; ask yourself what qualities the cannabis seems to embody. Hold a piece of ready to smoke herb in your hand and address the goddess. Invite the goddess within to manifest outwardly, and invite the goddess without to enter your body. Feel this same energy present in the herb as well. Touch the herb to your forehead, where the third eye chakra is located. Ask that your sight be opened; welcome the goddess to see through your eyes. Place the herb in a freshly cleaned glass bowl, and sit quietly as you smoke. Let your own thoughts drift away with each exhalation, and envision your third eye chakra spinning and glowing with each inhalation. When the bowl is finished, continue to sit quietly and open your mind to any impressions that are coming to you. If there is somewhere or someone you would like to psychically check in on, concentrate on the name of the person or place and note the visions you receive.

Hemp Charms

Here are a couple of charms that utilize the non-psychoactive hemp plant. Find hemp twine at arts and crafts store or online, and buy seeds at natural foods stores.

Solar Courage Talisman

Create and wear this talisman to magnify courage and to attract and absorb the solar qualities of the hemp plant. Get some hemp twine and cut off two pieces long enough to form a bracelet. Tie the two strings together at one end, then tie or pin this to something to hold it steady as you work. Cross one string over the other, bringing it around the underside and back up through the loop. Pull it tight until the knot moves to the top of the string. Continue making knots in this manner, tying one string around the other, until it is long enough to wrap around your wrist. Anoint the bracelet with frankincense oil or hemp oil, and then set it out in the sunshine. As you invite the sun into the bracelet, think of the strength of the hemp plant, thriving in harsh conditions, thinking of its powerful fibers and rapid growth. Envision yourself as being like the hemp, bold, unstoppable, and full of strength and energy. Feel your courage grow. Imagine yourself brimming with confidence as you bravely conquer a previously fear-inducing scenario. When the image is clear in your mind and your feeling of courage is at its height, direct the flow of power into the bracelet. Leave it out in the sun for a couple of hours, then retrieve it before sundown and tie it around your wrist.

Surround and Defend Charm

When foes threaten, here's a quick charm that can help protect yourself, your loved ones, or even the environment. Place an image of the person or place you wish to protect on your altar. Gaze at the image and conjure a protective energy from within you. Let your desire to defend and protect, your inner strength and power, increase and flow outward into the image. Now take a handful of hemp seeds and sprinkle them around the image in a circle. Be sure the circle is completely closed with no large gaps. Affirm out loud that the person or place is protected, surrounded by an impenetrable shield guarded by the god of the sun, the god of the hemp. Leave the charm in place until the danger has passed.

A Sacred Ally

With its many magickal and mundane uses, the cannabis plant is indeed a sacred ally. It's a truly beautiful plant, and like any magickal plant, it should be appreciated, honored, and utilized to its fullest potential. It's not all about getting stoned and numbed to daily stresses; it's about the magick, the love, the life this plant imparts.

Datura:
Trumpet of the Spirit Realm
By Christopher Penczak

y initiator, my teacher, my friend, and even my love: Dame Datura. Her flowers enticed me from the first moment we met, though she repulses just as many as she attracts. Like those of her family, the Solanaceae, there is great magick in her, and that magick attracts those seeking the mysteries, and repels those afraid of the dark. Along with Belladonna, Black Nightshade, Henbane, and Mandrake, Datura is known as one of the Witch's herbs. They are found in the classic Witch's Flying Ointment recipes, toxic balms that propel the Witch into the spirit realm to the Sabbat. Others in the same family are less ominous, including Potato, Tomato and Eggplant, as well as Tobacco.

Datura is known by many folk names, including Thorn Apple, Devil's Apple, Devil's Trumpet, Devil's Weed, Witch's Weed, Witch's Thimble, Hell's Bells, Stink Weed, Zombie-Cucumber, and Moon Flower. One of its most famous names is Jimson Weed, named after James Town, Virginia, as the inhabitants ate its dark green leaves and suffered the effects of its poison. Its name Datura comes from the *dhatūrā*, the Indian name of the plant, where it is also known as Sacred Datura. The colorful, and dark, names associated with the plant demonstrate a powerful link with the mysteries of the Witch.

Like many plant allies, I was introduced to Datura from a friend who had a potted plant. She knew it was associated with Witchcraft, but didn't know how to use it magickally and ritually. She knew it was associated with the teachings of Carlos Castaneda, from reading his first book, *The Teachings of Don Juan: A Yaqui Way of Knowledge*. The sorcerer could go one of two ways with a plant ally, given choice between the Little

Smoke, a mixture containing the Mexican psilocybin, teaching about the perception of time, or Datura, an ally that will teach spirit flight, divination, psychic perception and attraction, but it's a hard ally to tame. Datura is a jealous spirit. She demands your attention. For a male sorcerer, it's like a jealous lover.

She gave me the potted plant. Another friend, gaining a similar specimen, under the name Moon Flower, took instant revulsion to it and feared it would poison her children once she learned its true identity, as many different plants are known as Moon Flower. I, however, was fascinated and loved the presence of the plant. Some people, like me, find its scent intoxicating. Sometimes it is compared to a lemon scent, though I must admit that I don't smell lemon with it. Many consider the scent to be narcotic. Others find it like rotting meat, revolting. From that point on, I endeavored to learn all I could about Datura, both intellectually and spiritually. Sadly, due to its poisonous nature, there was not a lot of direct lore on how to use it safely chemically, but lots of references to it as an oracular herb, used in a wide variety of contexts, even beyond the "Witch's Weeds" of the flying ointment.

Datura is found all over the world, with a wide variety of species. It can be found as far as India and China, and down south in Peru. There is a variety of "Tree Datura" known as Brugmansia, which also goes by the name Angel Trumpet. Unlike many of the more traditional Datura species, it creates a woody bush or small tree, and its flowers hang down and are not erect. The eastern American species, Jimson Weed, is known as *Datura stramonium*. Its leaves are jagged and the flower has a slightly purple hue. Its seeds, within the spiky four section "apple," are black. The Datura of the Southwest and Mexico is *Datura inoxia*, with rounded leaves. Its seeds are brown and kidney shaped. There are several other forms of Datura, but those are the most used by American Witches today. Other species of Datura include: *Datura alba, Datura bernhardii, Datura ceratocaula, Datura discolor, Datura ferox, Datura insignis, Datura leichhardtii, Datura metel, Datura nanakai, Datura parajuli, Datura pruinosa, Datura quercifolia, Datura tatula, Datura wrightii.*

Datura inoxia flower

Datura Mythology

Datura has a mixed reputation in the lore, embodying both danger and duplicity, and enlightenment and the deepest spiritual journey. This mix shows its unpredictable nature. It can be used to cure or kill, to hex or unhex, and is often used to find spiritual allies and awaken inborn psychic powers. The root can also bring luck in gambling, and along with consuming the seeds, would increase the psychic powers to make better bets. Peruvians would chew on the root to conjure the spirits. Datura inoxia has been used among the Zuni to appeal to the spirits for rain. Datura reveals the location of lost objects and the origin and purpose of disease. Datura could help reveal the future and the identity of thieves. Many of the arts of the local Cunning Man of the village are enhanced by Datura, though it doesn't seem to have a lot of folkloric use in European traditions by such healers.

In a Zuni Datura legend, a small boy and girl, siblings named A'neglakya and A'neglakyatsi-tsa, lived deep inside the Earth. They would come up to the surface of the world to explore and take long walks. They carefully observed and listened to all things upon the Earth. When they returned, they told their parents everything they saw and heard. The pair was watched by the twin sons of the Sun god, who wondered what they were up to upon the world. They later encountered the twin gods, who asked how the boy and girl were doing. The boy, A'neglakya, told the two gods that he and his sister had the power to make people go to sleep and have dreams, or see where lost objects really were. Some say the two were eavesdropping on the sacred council of spirits, and in turn were going to share what secrets they heard with their parents. Upon the advice of the twins of the Sun god, they were sent back into the Earth, never to return, but from where they sank, two Datura plants grew. The gods called the flower A'neglakya and spread them across the Earth. Now, those who partake in the

Datura as a sacrament, but risk its danger, can also listen to the sacred council of spirits.

Datura metel is an important herb to the Chumash people of California. They believe their ancestor, one of the First People of the world, a grandmother known as Momoy, had the gift of clairvoyance. When the great flood came, she became a Datura plant. Those who have her as sacrament, in the form of a cold water tea, can share in her gifts. It is used in initiation rituals of those reaching puberty, boys solitary and girls in small groups. Through a cold water infusion of the root, the initiate experiences communion with a protective animal spirit. When returning from the sleeping vision, the initiate is explained the vision and given the tribal history, ethics, and morals. The experience makes these things go deep within the consciousness. Initiates can visit with Momoy when they so choose.

Datura was used by the Algonquins in their male initiation ceremonies. Creating a potion known as wysocean, it was given continuously for about twenty days during the initiation ceremony. These boys would "unlive" their childhood memories, forgetting their boyhood to become men. Some believe the plant used by the Algonquin tribe was Datura tatula, lilac colored flowers with purple stems. Many consider it to be a variety of Datura stramonium, while others see it as a different species.

As many power plants are also associated with animal spirits, Datura is classically associated with the Owl, another feminine archetype with a mixed reputation, and the moth. Moths are most likely to pollinate the flowers, and some moths and butterflies eat the datura leaves. The Hopi word *tsimonmana* (plural: *tsimonmanant*) refers to both moths and the Jimson Weed, and usually is translated as Jimson Weed Maidens, showing up in Hopi Art. The Jimsonweed itself is sometimes depicted as a man with the seedpod for a body. Beetles, totems of death and rebirth, are also associated with it. Along with owls, moths, and beetles, keepers of the flying mysteries, wolves are also associated with Datura. It is said that wolf is the protective manifestation, and when you approach without respect, it approaches you like a wolf and tears you apart. If you approach in the right frame, it manifests as a flying creature and takes you on an enlightening journey. Some perceive the canine creature not as a wolf, but a black dog, which is common in Witchcraft myths. The dog/wolf is to test you, and if you are unflinching and respectful, it will let you pass. Shapeshifting into birds is a common flight experience with Datura as well. While Owls are traditional, I've found crow, raven and eagle also possible when working with it. Don Juan used it to shapeshift into a crow.

Don Juan compared Datura to an unhealthy relationship with a woman, believing she gives power too easily to control a man, distorting him. He felt use of Datura made men weak, even though his own teacher chose Datura over the "little smoke." In many ways, he describes the classic negative attributes of the Venus archetype, and western magicians associate this family of plants with both Venus, as a feminine aphrodisiac, and Saturn, for death. He did have some useful instructions on how to work with Datura if you chose to.

He suggested using the entire plant – roots, leaves, flowers, and seeds. I prefer to use the root as a charm, and only the seeds and leaves in magickal work. Each part is said to have its own power that must be "conquered." His method of divination with lizards is unusual and cruel if carried out literally. One wonders if it is meant to be symbolic, as one lizard is sent forth, while the other is upon the sorcerer's shoulder whispering secrets that the wandering lizard is perceiving.

One should always ask permission of the plant before working with it. Iron should never be used to dig it up, only the branch of a "tree-friend." This is common in a lot of faery folk lore. Iron should not touch the plant, or it will harm it, and drain its natural powers and blessings. Iron is baneful to the faery ladies. If you are friendly to the Datura, the Datura will be helpful and well-disposed to you.

One of the Central or South American daturas is also known as Toloache, and has been added to Ayahuasca brews. It's unclear if Toloache refers specifically to Brugmansia, or the more standard form of Datura, particularly Datura inoxia. In the Mexican Catholic Church, its patron is Santo Tolache, the patron saint for those seeking love. Datura flowers and tea are a sacrament.

In South America, both the Auruks and the Jivaros make a brew from various species to give to their children, believing the spirit of the plant will tame unruly children and teach them respect. The Jivaro people believe that initiation use of Brugmansia can give one an "outer soul" what we might call the Body of Light in western magick, to commune with the ancestral spirit. Datura fastuosa was used in Africa by virgin boys, who would, under its direction, act as a psychic detective, revealing the culprit of a crime in the village.

Datura was said to be used in the Caribbean as an ingredient to the Zombie formula, giving it the name Zombie-Cucumber. Along with the pufferfish poison, the main active ingredient, a criminal would be turned into a zombie to serve a sorcerer. Regular doses of Datura was said to maintain the state of compliance. On a magical level, it is said to send forth the spirit of the victim, from the body, making the state of "flight" permanent.

Dhatūrā, in India, refers to the dhat, the eternal essence of the divine. It is associated with the supreme god, the dissolver, Shiva, and is a symbol of enlightenment and death. Shiva is the dancer of time and space, the great destroyer and transformer in the Hindu trinity of Brahma, Vishnu, and Shiva. He is associated with Shakti, Durga, and Kali as his consort. Kali is depicted as standing or dancing upon his slumbering body. Datura was said to grow out of Lord Shiva's chest. While his devotees smoke cannabis, most do not smoke datura in worship, but offer the seedpods on festival days. Datura flowers are offered to Shiva on the 13th day of the waxing Moon in January. For those that do smoke Datura, the trumpet is said to be male, while the cannabis is female. The mix of the two balances duality. The blend is said to awaken the kundalini at the base of the spine, and resolve all duality and paradox, bringing one into enlightenment. Datura is also associated with the Thugee cult of Kali. Supposedly it was used to bestow fearlessness upon the thugs when they attacked their victims, and to drug their ritual sacrifices.

Datura the Plant

No one is quite sure where in the world Datura originates. It is found in Asia, Africa, and the Americas. Some think explorers of the New world brought Datura back to Europe, while others think its origin is near the Caspian Sea and traveled with gypsies, the Romani, through Europe.

Datura appears to like disturbed soil, and grows in waste fields, construction sites, and road sides quite readily. The Southwestern form grows well in the sandy stretches of land, while the eastern Stramonium likes richer soil. The fused five petalled trumpet-like blossoms of most species yield a thorny seed pod. The pods break open and scatter the seeds. According to Carlos Castaneda, all plants that grow from a sorcerer's plant, washed away, also belong to the sorcerer, no matter how far they go. It blooms at night and can wither away by morning, making it a flower for those night walkers. The flowers, like all five petalled flowers, are reminiscent of the pentagram.

Datura contains what are known as the belladonna alkaloids, atropine, scopolamine, and hyoscyamine. They are considered poisons as they inhibit acetylcholine when they pass the blood-brain barrier. Toxic doses can induce blurred vision, agitation, nausea, vertigo, hysteria or hysterical laughter, fevers, delirium, dehydration, intense arousal, cramps, painful urination, and memory loss. The memory loss can be permanent in some people. Datura is considered the most dangerous herb, perhaps along with Belladonna, to use recreationally or take internally, as the level of chemicals in the plant vary from time, place, and growing conditions, making a standard dose impossible to determine. While there is a lot of hysteria around Datura, it's not unfounded, as there are reports of severe poisoning and deaths attributed to the plant.

In the past Datura has been used as a sedative and pain reliever. Tincture of Datura is used to sedate patients for more primitive forms of surgery. In India it is used as a cure for asthma, smoked in cigarette form to relieve the symptoms of the disease.

Datura seeds are placed in alcoholic drinks, from the Brugmansia species used in corn beer of South America, to wine in China and beer in Europe in the Middle Ages. Chinese lore associates Datura alba, or Man-t'o-lo with the pole stars. They too mixed it with cannabis and wine. In South America, it was administered as an enema or leaf suppository. Some use various forms of Datura in ointments for aches, pains, rashes, swelling, cracked skin, and wounds. Makes me wonder what the recovery period is like for the patient.

For the Jamestown poisoning, it was in a soup that the soldiers ate. While reports said they were dazed for eleven days, acting outrageously, usually it will either kill or leave the system in twenty-four hours, so perhaps the reports were slightly exaggerated over time.

Datura ceratocaula, also known as Atlinan among the Aztecs, is considered the "sister" to the Ololuiqui plant, another entheogen. It's a flowering vine akin to Morning Glory.

Visions induced by Datura often tend to be of a sexual nature. It is considered to be an aphrodisiac of the highest order, but an obviously dangerous one. Physical arousal is one of the effects of the plants, as many of the belladonna alkaloids have this tendency. Datura, both magickally and due to its narcotic properties, can be used in love potions and philters to bewitch someone into sensual mesmerism.

Navajo cautionary advice on Datura "Eat a little, and go to sleep. Eat some more, and have a dream. Eat some more, and don't wake up." Sound advice to remember when working with any of the plants from this family. Many believe she doesn't want to be ingested, but worked with through cultivation and dreams. Even touching Datura can cause a reaction in some people. Other believe she must instruct you if she is to be taken as a sacrament prior, through dreams and visions. To those she invites, she is gentle and gives knowledge of how to use her. To those she does not invite, she offers only death.

Just like with other entheogens, as Timothy Leary taught, the set and setting, as well as the dose, influence the experience greatly. Fasting before working with Datura internally is a common practice, as is sexual abstinence. Many entheogenic traditions suggest both practices. One is due to the nausea induced, so less food in the system is better, and helps induce altered states anyway, requiring less plant matter, and other because Datura and many other plant spirits are jealous lovers at times. Since Datura often invokes a sexual reaction, she wants that energy for her relationship with you. Abstinence can also generally build up life force for the ritual, while sexuality activity, when not careful, depletes life force.

Datura should never be taken by those with any heart conditions, pregnant or lactating women, nor those suffering from consumption, depression, infection, or mental illness. If overdosed, one should vomit and seek a hospital. There is no cure for Datura poisoning, and stomach pumping is necessary, though a preparation of activated willow charcoal can help prevent further absorption, detoxifying the body.

Working with Datura

To maintain safety, I worked with Datura as a flower essence. As a dilute solution of the flowers, preserved in water, is quite safe to take orally, or use in ritual. Datura essence helps us with both communing with the dead and letting go of people who have passed on from this life. Datura can also be helpful in letting go when you are transitioning, but fear to leave the world. Datura eases all transitions and shifts of reality and identity, particularly when great fear is brought up, or potential for delusions arise. It eases the delusions. It helps us perceive reality in new ways, from visionary experiences to more mundane perception shifts. It can help you see and hear messages from your intuition and spirit guides. Those who suffer from life shattering experiences and traumas are aided in readjusting.

I used Datura essence in rituals for the ancestors, particularly for Samhain, and to help myself and others deepen connections to spirit guides and deities of the underworld. Datura is associated with the Moon, the Goddess and the spirits of darkness. I used drops of it in the chalice for the Great Rite in my Full and Dark Moon rituals. Despite its darker associations, many also connect it to the realm of the angels and archangels, and I've had powerful experiences with it. As it's ruled by Venus and Saturn, the archangels Haniel (Venus) Tzafkiel (Saturn) and Uriel (Earth) resonate best with it.

My experience with Datura deepened when I was ill for an extended period of time. I contracted pneumonia, and couldn't shake it. After trying western medicine and herbalism, I thought I would try working with a homeopath. She was a Witch too, so I felt totally comfortable working with her. She used homeopathic remedies in her magick, and while she was well versed in them, she was not as well versed with the living plants. So after a very long in-take session, asking me a wide range of questions, she told me she would have to "dream on it" to tell me what was my core, vital remedy, though she had some ideas. The next day, she told me the homeopathic remedy that would boost my life force was Stramonium. At the time, I was less well versed in plant species, but it sounded familiar. Stramonium.... stramonium.... what was that? We looked it up in a homeopathic materia medica, and found that it was Devil's Trumpet, Thorn Apple, or Jimson Weed. All names I was far more familiar with. Perfect. A plant I already had a deep spiritual connection with, turned out to be my homeopathic ally. Stramonium is used for restlessness, nightmares, anxiety, fear of the dark, fevers and delusions, as the poisoning of Jimson Weed causes all those symptoms. Homeopathic remedies work with "like cures like." While I wasn't suffering from those symptoms specifically, I do suffer from a general restlessness all the time, particularly at night. She felt that Stramonium really best matched my personality, the expression of my life force, and as a remedy would help boost me in all things. I started taking it and made a dramatic improvement in three days. I take it regularly, and as needed, to help bolster my own energy and it's been an amazing way to work with it.

Shortly before my homeopathic experience, a Hermetic magician well versed in entheogenic substances sent me a package. An old friend, who knew I was a Witch, but not necessarily of my connection with Datura, was growing Datura. At the end of the growing cycle, when cutting back plants, the spent annual of the Datura told him that the root was for me, so I received a long root in the mail. I meditated with it, to commune with the plant spirit, as that year, my Daturas in the garden did not do so well. They need lots of light, and prefer disturbed soil. The growth spurts of a tree lessened the only full Sun area of my garden. I guess I was too excited, as I held the fragile root too hard, and it snapped into three pieces. In the meditation, a little shocked but still present, I received instructions to wrap each piece in thread – white, red, and black – and then bind them together with a thread braided of white, red and black. Then it got strange. The female voice told me to rub it with the oil of my favorite healing herb – Lemon Balm – and then anoint it with sexual fluids. Sleep with it under my pillow to receive deeper healing and instructions. I did. And I was visited by a lady with beautiful long white hair wearing a white shimmering dress, who has taught me many things. Further into our relationship, I saw her sharp nails and teeth, akin to the spikes of the Datura pods. Later, speaking to some friends on a more Traditional Craft path, I discovered this was not such an unusual technique with the baneful herbs. While Datura's myths and legends are sometimes male, more often than not, it is associated with a feminine goddess spirit, sometimes aggressive or cold in its bluntness. It can be compared to figures such as Kali or Hecate by modern mythologist, though Datura tends to be more sexual in nature than Hecate is usually depicted.

One of the most important lessons Dame Datura told me was her magick in opening the worlds, and how she differed from her sister, Belladonna. Belladonna has appeared to me almost as her inverse, dark haired, dark eyes, and dressed in deep purple. Datura told me that she is the sister who opens the gates of spirit vertically, while her sibling opens them horizontally. If you have wings, meaning you can journey already, you can fly with Datura to the heavens, to the over world, as well as the depths. Those who try to use her recreationally, for "fun" usually report horrifically unpleasant experiences. They are either visited by the dead, zombies, or all sorts of monsters. These people cannot "fly" so they fall into "hell" when she opens the gates. The dead are the first layer of the underworld, and often the dead who are trapped near the world, but not in it, are unpleasant.

Datura not only told me that she opens the gates, but she also awakens the crown and third eye, and that is part of her medicine in teaching us to deal with death through our connection to the spirit world. As the spirit world is accessible via the dream world, she is also a powerful ally in dream work. Through this all, she helps us face our fears, conscious and unconscious. The spikes are described like knives wielded by the Datura plant spirit, helping dissect thoughts, feelings, motives, and energy. When we move through our fears, we can be more heart centered, commune with our deeper self, and through this peace, find out who we are and what our purpose is.

Ritually, use of Datura is frowned upon because of its danger. While it is very dangerous, I think they are acceptable ways to work with it. Datura leaves and seeds are traditionally smoked in cigarettes and burned in incense, much like tobacco. Sadly I don't find Datura smokes as well as tobacco. I used the ground leaves and seeds in incense, burned upon charcoal. Saturnine herbs work well with Datura incense. A simple recipe to use Datura is:

3 Tablespoons Mugwort
1 Tablespoon Myrrh
1 Tablespoon Red Sandalwood
1 Tablespoon Datura Leaves
¼ Tablespoon Datura Seeds
10 Drops Myrrh Oil
5 Tablespoons of Warm Wine
1 Tablespoon of Honey

Mix the dry ingredients together as a powder. Add the liquids and mix thoroughly. Let it dry out and crumble into chunks. Burn small chunks on charcoal. Don't inhale directly, but let the smoke diffuse in the temple space. If you have concerns about poisoning, keep the area well ventilated.

Datura can be used orally as a tea. I suggest using the seeds, not the leaves or flowers, as the seeds have a more consistent chemical level of alkaloids. I suggest using applied kinesiology, or muscle testing, to determine a safe threshold dose. For those unfamiliar with muscle testing, I suggest my book, *The Inner Temple of Witchcraft,* for a crash course in this form of body divination. Don't try more than seven seeds to start. My usual threshold dose is around five seeds. Crush the seeds in a mortar and pestle. Add a small bit of ginger, lemon balm, or honey with the seeds, to a cup of hot water, and let it steep for a few hours. Ginger helps any nausea problems. Drink a good half hour to hour before your ritual. I've found this dose doesn't induce solid visions, but enhances any visionary work, for those who know "how to fly."

I also like to use Datura as an oil. Crush nine seeds in a mortar and pestle, and add to a base oil, such as jojoba or grape seed oil. Use a dram, or twenty drops. Leave the vial of oil with crushed seeds exposed to the Full Moon light. Anoint the back of the head, at the top of the spine/base of the skull, what is known as the altar major chakra, and anoint the brow. This Datura oil will help enhance magickal visions and spirit contact. Some would use the oil mixed with beeswax as a base for an ointment. You can add a variety of essential oils to help enhance. A few drops of Myrrh, Lemon Balm, Angelica, Ylang-Ylang, or Sandalwood will enhance the blend.

Any use of Datura as a visionary herb is complimented through ritual. I've found rituals with sensual touches – music, other scents, dance, and such, in a slow, rhythmic and hypnotic pace can facilitate the process. Less Datura is required, making it safer, and the experience in the ritual setting makes it more profound.

Ritual magick with Datura, without ingestion or topical application, can include psychic enhancement, dream magick, love and lust magick, protection magick due to the thorns, dark goddess communication, faery contact, healing, blessing, and cursing. Carry the leaves, root, or seeds in a charm bag. In the Ozark mountain magickal traditions, the leaves can be placed in the hat to protect the wearer against sunstroke. The flowers can be steeped in alcohol with rose and other Venusian herbs to create a perfume to entice and seduce. Daniel A. Shulke, in his grimoire *Viridarium Umbris,* offers a formula of Datura blossom, rose, and cured tobacco. It can be placed upon letters and other objects touched by the intended recipient of the magick.

One of the most effective and safe ways to work deeply with the spirit of Datura, beyond flower essences, homeopathy, and herbal preparations, is to grow Datura yourself. The cultivation of the plant, growing the seeds, watering the plants, and smelling the flowers, is very powerful. Often you can meditate beneath the flowers without even picking them or touching them and have an amazing effect. Dreaming beneath Datura flowers is very powerful, but safe. Those seeking to harvest the seeds and fearful they will be lost upon the wind, my friends Joe and Doug from Otherworld Apothecary suggest putting a muslin tea bag around the pod. When it opens, the seeds fall into the bag. Root charms like my own can be made for deepening your contact off season.

Seek out Dame Datura when you are looking for an ally through the fear, to find true vision of the spirit world, and your purpose. While she might be tough to "tame" as Carlos said, I would suggest not trying to tame her, but honor her as the wise woman she is.

Sources

DeKorne, Jim. *Psychedelic Shamanism: The Cultivation, Preparation and Shamanic Use of Psychotropic Plants.* Loompanics Unlimited, Port Townsend, WA: 1994. 2002, revised edition.

Harvey, Clare G. and Amanda Cochrane. *The Healing Spirit of Plant: A Practical Guide to Plant Spirit Medicine.* Sterling Publishing Co., Inc. New York, NY: 2001.

Safford, William Edwin. *Daturas of the Old World and New: An account of their Narcotic Properties and their use in Oracular and Initiatory Ceremonies* (1922). Washington Government Printing Office: 1922.

Shulke, Daniel A. *Viridarium Umbris.* Xoanon Publishing. Cheshire, England: 2005.

http://www.alchemy-works.com/datura_info.html

http://www.alchemy-works.com/datura_inoxia.html

http://www.alchemy-works.com/datura_stramonium.html

http://paultkay.info/DATURA_05_08_2006.pdf

http://www.saguaro-juniper.com/i_and_i/flowers/datura/datura.html

http://www.angelfire.com/indie/anna_jones1/datura.html

http://en.wikipedia.org/wiki/Datura_stramonium

http://www.erowid.org/plants/datura/datura_info7.shtml

http://b-and-t-world-seeds.com/Datura.htm

http://www.xplanta.com/46/datura-tatula/

http://www.xplanta.com/47/datura-stramonium/

Diviner's Sage

By Darryl McGlynn

"Few have heard of it. Fewer know what it looks like. Fewer still have ever met the sagely ally, yet the alliance forms invisible links wherever it goes..."

— Dale Pendell, *Pharmako/Poeia*

here are many species in the genus Salvia, and Diviner's Sage is the most prolific. The hidden knowledge that the "Sage of the Seers" can grant is tremendous and I am thrilled to share my experiences with you.

Diviner's Sage is a green lover that is used to facilitate mind altering experiences. It is known to the Mazatec Indians of Mexico and said to be used in their "medico-magico" divinatory ceremonies. In the late 1930s, these rituals first came to the minds of North American anthropologists but it was not until 1962 that this plant fell into their hands. Diviner's Sage has many names including the Sage of the Seers, Salvia divinorum or simply, Salvia. It is the most psychoactive of the salvias. It is used as a means to achieve altered states of consciousness in which different perceptions, unhindered by everyday mental filters and processes, can arise. It is commonly used in modern shamanic practices as a "legal" replacement of other psychedelics. Those who use Diviner's Sage in this way believe that its mind-altering effect, combined with a specific intent, can be life altering and are not mere hallucinations. While some aspects of the experience may be hallucinations, the mental and emotional awareness that is felt is real. It is those very human experiences that are opened within, that lift the veil and separate ordinary reality from alternative landscapes. Diviner's Sage allows the gateway of the nierika to open and the consciousness to expand into the spiritual realm.

I first heard about this herb, during a conversation concerning the ability to produce altered states without the use of "illegal" psychedelics. I explained that I am not opposed to people who use such substances but I was on a path that could not allow for it. Namely, my career has protocols in place to test for the use of illegal drugs. A friend explained that Diviner's Sage or, as he called it, Salvia, is technically not illegal but not really legal. He went on to explain that Salvia is sort of in a gray area that you cannot get into trouble if you have it, but you are frowned upon if you are caught with it. Salvia divinorum remains legal in most countries today. In Canada and the United States it is controlled though. In 2002 the United States legislated that Diviner's Sage, or its active ingredient salvinorin A, should be placed under a schedule I controlled substance. This went under bill HR 5607, but was not passed. Though it is not regulated at the federal level, some states have passed their own laws against Salvia including Alabama, Delaware, Louisiana, Michigan, Missouri, and Ohio. Where these laws do exist, Salvia varies in its prohibitive degree. So please check the individual state laws and regulations about this plant before you obtain it!

Most plants have a round stem that is filled with "stuff". Not Diviner's Sage, it has a hollow square stem. When cut across and looked at from the tip, it reveals its true mystery, the circle within a square! In witchcraft, the casting of our circle is considered our sacred space, in which we are protected from unwanted energies. It is a temple that is a space beyond space, a time beyond time. The square represents the material world, the four elements manifested fully in our realm. The circle is the sign of our divinity while the square is the symbol of our physicality. To the Qabalist, the circle within a square is a symbol for the spark of divinity residing within the material realm. Thus we see the true nature of Diviner's Sage as a plant to awaken that divine spark within us.

The leaves have no hair, are large with yellow undertones, and can grow up to 30 cm long in perfect conditions. The plant itself can grow up to 1 meter in height. It has flowers but they rarely bloom. If you are lucky enough to experience this, they can be described as blue flowers, crowned with a white dome. They grow to be about 3 cm with six flowers to each dome. When it does bloom, most of the time in its native habitat, it does so from September to May.

Salvinorin A is the main active psychotropic in Salvia divinorum. Since it contains no nitrogen atoms, it is distinct from other "natural" hallucinogens, such as DMT and mescaline. Depending on the method of ingestion, Salvinorin A can produce psychoactive experiences with a duration being several minutes to an hour. The chemical formula is $C_{23}H_{28}O_8$, and without nitrogen found in its makeup, Salvinorin A is not an alkaloid. Salvinorin A, is the most potent "naturally occurring" hallucinogen. If the pure drug is smoked at high concentration, it is detectable in urine for the first hour. However, 1½ hours after smoking it, the levels would be well below the detection limit.

When growing your own Diviner's Sage, I found it best to use small pots and repot as the plant grows. I used loose soil with drainage at the bottom of the pot. I live on a horse farm and we use peat moss to bed down the horses, so the mixture of horse manure and peat moss is what I used. Though it was not the fresh stuff, I used the older decomposed stuff out back! I regularly watered and kept the plant in direct sunlight. When I was away, I left the plant in an area that allowed the greatest amount of sunlight. When I was home, I would literally move the pot around so that it would have continuous sunlight. With this method of daily watering and the continual sunlight, it created a good amount of moisture. Even though I live north of Toronto Canada, which is a long way from the Mexican environment, my plant grew to be about 1 ½ feet tall! Its leaves must have been 4 inches long and 2 inches wide but sadly, it did not flower. Later, I found these soil mixtures:

Mixture One
1 part aged grass cuttings
1 part compost
1 part coarse sand
½ part aged steer manure
3 parts rich soil

Mixture Two
2 five-gallon buckets coconut "coir" fiber (or substitute black peat)
1 bucket coarse sand
1 bucket vermiculite
1 bucket perlite
1 bucket rich soil
1 bucket compost
6 cups of an equal part blend of organic nutrients: colloidal phosphate, greensand, and bloodmeal
¼ cup ground limestone (double if using peat)

Mixture Three
4 parts soil
2 parts peat moss
1 part vermiculite
1 part perlite

With these mixtures, you can experiment and create your own based on the conditions in your environment. I would suggest reading the *Salvia Divinorum Growers Guide* if this is a plant you want to include on your green lovers list. It contains great tips on other soil practices that you may find interesting to note, including pH levels and temperatures. If you are like me, I do not like to use chemicals to control pest in my gardens. Here is a simple formula that you can use to control them, that is environmentally friendly!

Mix together:
4 parts water
1 part rubbing alcohol
1 part liquid castile soap

Sage is a sacred ceremonial herb. It is associated with immortality and is known to increase mental capacity. It is believed that it can cure disease from the body by easing the strain on the heart. People drink sage tea to treat colds, fevers, liver trouble, epilepsy, memory loss, and many other common afflictions. Sage also has antibacterial properties. Sage has been used as a beauty aid applying it to the body or bathing in sage tea. It can be used as a natural hair dye for gray hair and it still is recommended for use in dark hair today. Just like salt and pepper are everyday spices, in old times sage was commonplace. Its use today during Thanksgiving has become a popular American tradition. There is an old Arab belief that if your sage grows well, you will live a long time. During the fourteenth century, three leaves a day were to be eaten to avoid the "evil air". Sage was also a favorite of the Hungarian gypsies; they believed that it attracted good and dispelled evil. *Salvia Apiana,* or white sage, is commonly used by Native Americans in their smudge pots as incense. In modern culture, salvia divinorum is more widely known and used than any other natural psychedelic. Approximately 1 million people in the US alone use it. In magickal practices, Diviner's Sage is used to replace the "other substances that can bring trouble to your doorstep". Living a magickal life as a witch is hard enough for some of us. Various methods of ingestion include smoking, chewing the leaf (also called quid chewing), or creating a tincture. Through the various means of consumption I have tried, I found the effects to include:

- Spontaneous past life regressions
- Feeling of being pulled or contorted by an outside force
- Merging with objects
- "Bilocation" (being in two different locations at the same time).

Smoking

I have read that the temperature that is needed to release the active ingredient, Salvinorin A, is very high, so the use of a torch lighter is recommended. You can use your pipe but the smoke can be very hot so many times people use a "water pipe" to cool the smoke. If you grow the plant yourself, when harvesting the leaves, you must put them out to dry before smoking them. Because it is natural, you will never know the amount of the Salvinorin A concentration in the leaves, therefore, most prefer to purchase Diviner's Sage extracts. These are usually labeled with a number and then an "x", noting the multiplication levels of the Salvinorin A concentration i.e. 5x, 10x, and so on. This should not be taken as absolute because there is no accepted standard for this rating process.

Chewing

Salvinorin A is somewhat deactivated by the gastrointestinal system, so orally ingesting it would probably not produce any strong or lasting effect. Holding the "quid" of the leaves in your mouth and allowing it to be absorbed through your oral membranes produces a greater effect. This is manner in which "chewing tobacco" is used. "Quid" refers to the fact that at the end of this method the user spits out the leaves rather than swallowing them. I have found that chewing Diviner's Sage produces a longer lasting experience than smoking it.

Tincture

This not a common practice, but I use it regularly. This method allows for a multitude of uses, including drinking it, placing drops on paper for magickal use, and cleansing specific magickal tools. You can create a simple tea out of the leaves to drink by crushing them to extract the juices. However, between 20 and 80 fresh leaves would be needed. These juices can then be mixed with water to create an infusion, which when ingested would grant visions. Another option is the alchemist's process for the creation of elixirs and tinctures. These are made with alcohol. If needed, the tincture can be diluted with water to lessen the "stinging" sensation. I usually use a dropper and place one or two drops under my tongue. When taken as a tincture, the effects can range from inducing a mild meditative state to bringing about a more intense visionary one and its duration is similar to other methods of oral ingestion. Here is the process I use to create my tinctures.

Herbal Elixir
High quality alcohol
Mortar and pestle
2 glass canning jars with lids
Plastic wrap
Funnel
Cheesecloth
Heat proof glass dish with lid
Metal spoon
Airtight jar
Book of matches
Diviner's Sage leaves

Using the mortar and pestle, grind enough of the herb into a fine powder to fill a canning jar 1/3 full. Add the alcohol (151 or 190 proof) to fill the jar. Place a piece of plastic wrap over the jar then seal it with its lid. Place this jar in a warm, moist area where you can shake it thoroughly at least once a day for a minimum of 2 weeks, however, 6 weeks is preferred. Pour the mixture into the second canning jar using the funnel and cheesecloth to separate the herbs and the liquid. Seal the jar of liquid using the plastic wrap and its lid. This liquid is what the alchemists call the sulfur and mercury component that heals the spiritual and soul levels of the individual. This is the tincture you can use! Remove the herb from the cheesecloth and place it in the heatproof glass dish. Take it outside and touch it with a lit match setting it on fire and burning off any excess alcohol. Stir it with a metal spoon to make sure all the alcohol burns off. Bake this herb in your oven at 500 degrees for at least an hour or until it is reduced to a gray white ash. This process can create a lot of smoke. Let the ash cool and then place it in the airtight jar. This is what the alchemists call the salt component that heals the physical body. This healing process can be done by placing a pinch of the ash into a glass of water to drink or over your food, as you would regular table salt.

Witches use different types of herbs to cleanse or consecrate their tools. Choosing the herbs that resonate with what you are consecrating the tool for is a well-known practice. In the past I have been taught to use powerful herbs like, marijuana, for consecrating a tool that I would use to increase psychic abilities. Well, I was, and am still not, comfortable with the legal matters of those substances, so I have been delighted to find this green lover. I have used it in various rituals and spells. One particular spell that comes to mind is the one I performed with my crystal skull. It had such a long lasting effect on my relationship with my crystal skull, as well as myself, that I would like to share it with you. If you do not have a crystal skull that is okay, you can perform this spell with any crystals you may have.

Calling the Crystal Skull

First, create the ash and tincture using the method of the alchemist. You should have your crystal skull, ash, and tincture ready. Sit crossed-legged facing north. Place the crystal skull, sitting on a bed of the ash, in front of you facing east. Now say:

I call to the divine
The first mother, the first father and the ALL
I ask that you bless the skull, ash and tincture
So that they answer my call

Anoint your first and second fingers, on both hands, by touching them to the tincture. Use the fingers on your right hand to touch the top of your head, the crown chakra, while the fingers of your left hand touch your forehead, the brow chakra. Leaving them in this position say:

With this green lover
I awaken my own skull
With the ability to receive
The messages of my call

Close your eyes and take a few deep breaths. Feel the energy of your crown and brow chakra awakening. Now place your hands in the same manner on the crystal skull. Meditate here for a moment using exercise 13, Mental Projection, found in *The Inner Temple of Witchcraft* (page 134). Instead of holding the object in your hands, perform it from your current position. Focus on the point at which your fingers are touching the skull. Feel your consciousness moving through your arms and fingers and into the skull. When you feel the awareness of the skull, using your own words, call to its spirit to awaken and form a link with you. When you feel ready, thank the skull and its spirit. Now place your hands on your lap; open your eyes and say:

This link is now formed
Between myself and the spirit of the crystal skull
This bond will grow stronger with time
Through every message, with every call
So mote it be

Afterward, thank the divine, and do any necessary grounding that is needed. Place the skull facing the area or item that you would like it to watch over for you. I found that regularly performing this spell created a stronger bond, and I would receive messages when the area or item was disturbed. Though most of the time it was my cats that were nosing around and this would trigger the call! I found that when sitting and meditating on my crystal skull I could call to it and "see" through its eyes! It acted like a pair of "astral glasses" that I could use to see the area or item it was looking at, no matter where I was.

There are many ways to induce trance and many herbs that can aid in this process. But the green lover that is the easiest, safest, and legal one of them all is Diviner's Sage. The hidden knowledge that can be obtained through its use can be endless. If you are on a path, like me, that does not include the use of illegal substances, then the "Sage of the Seers" is the green lover for you.

Sources
Salvinorin—The Psychedelic Essence of Salvia Divinorum by D.M. Turner.

The Controlled Substances Act, USA.

The Salvia Divinorum Grower's Guide By Sociedad Para La Preservation De Las Plantas Del Misterio.

http://www.crucible.org/salvia_divinorum.htm: October 2011.

http://www.iamshaman.com/salvia/diviners-sage.htm#Legal_status:
October 2011.

http://en.wikipedia.org/wiki/Salvia_divinorum: October 2011.

Dragon's Blood: Resin of Power

By Christopher Penczak

When I first got involved in Witchcraft and saw potion formulas with the ingredient Dragon's Blood, I laughed. I had entered into the craft a skeptic, and while I loved the romance of potions and charms, the scientist in me, finally accepting of psychic reality and meditation, still thought the ritual magick portion of our teachings was a bit hokey. Dragon's Blood read to me like something out of a *Dungeons & Dragons* book, make believe. Where would one get a dragon? I like to share that whenever teaching a class on potions now, as Dragon's Blood has become one of my favorite ingredients.

Like many other folk names for plants, Dragon's Blood is named after an animal, or in this case, a more mythic or spiritual animal, because it has qualities relating to it. Many Witches today believe the old style recipes popularized in Shakespeare, such as eye of newt or bat wings were code for herbs. Juniper is considered newt eye and holly as bat wing. In modern surviving folk names, we still have some animal characteristics, such as Deer's Tongue. Though some will argue Witchcraft involves a system of healing and medicine akin to the more commonly accepted Ayurveda of India and Traditional Chinese Medicine (TCM), both of which are known to use animal parts in their elixirs and preparations. But I think it's safe to say that Dragon's Blood refers to a plant, not animal substance, in modern Witchcraft.

Dragon's Blood is a powerful red resin that actually refers to quite a number of different plants. The one used most often in occult recipes, particularly for incense, is *Daemonorops draco*. The substance comes from the fruit of this palm tree. Other plants referred to as Dragon's Blood include the genera *Croton*, *Dracaena*, *Calamus rotang*, and *Pterocarpus*. Along with

Deamonorops, Dracaena shows up in occult supplies. Many make no distinction between the different species called Dragon's Blood, though they have some different properties. Anything bright red in the ancient world, carrying a power, could be called Dragon's Blood, including the chemical cinnabar, which is toxic.

Before Dragon's Blood was available through occult suppliers, one had to find sources for it through violin shops, as it's used as a stain and varnish for violins. Laurie Cabot tells a wonderful story of trying to obtain Dragon's Blood from a violin maker in Boston, who feared she was starting a competitive business. When she revealed she wanted to use it as incense, and had also been frequenting the Catholic supply shops for frankincense and myrrh, the violin maker was happy to sell her small quantities of the red resin. Laurie's own teacher, a British witch named Felicity, used these ingredients in her magick, but did not reveal her suppliers and sources and Laurie only came back to her Craft later in life, receiving her original training as a teenager.

In occult and modern shamanic traditions, Dragon's Blood is seen as a power plant. It is a hard resin that burns well as incense, though larger chunks can be difficult to crush and powder. As it gets warmer it gets gummy, making powdering even more difficult, so some suggest freezing it first before attempting to pulverize it. I suggest placing it in a bag and then striking it with a hammer outdoors.

I learned that a pinch of Dragon's Blood added to anything would enhance the power of the magickal spell, potion, or formula. Its releases a powerful vibration, adding strength to all workings. It is a magickal catalyst, akin to Mandrake, Mistletoe, Tobacco, Vanilla, Licorice, and Lobelia. Just a pinch is needed. Ruled by Mars, due to its red color, and associated with fire as a dragon would be, Dragon's Blood is for victory and success. It is used in protection magick, and said when burned, to be one of the most powerful substances for exorcism. It banishes or destroys harmful spirits and energies. It can be used in love and lust spells for arousal and sexuality. In New Orleans Voodoo it is used for money and love drawing charms. Used in potions and oils that are topically applied, such as protection potion, I would not suggest using Dragon's Blood internally unless working with other species with better established medicinal virtues, though most are associated with astringent and wound healing virtues, such as the *Croton lechleri (Croton draco)* of South America.

While it can be burned alone to release a wonderful smell and powerful magick, as it is scentless dry, it works well in conjunction with other plants, as it enhances their power. Even though I happen to love the scent, its vibration will cast out harmful spirits. Much more pleasant than burning something like Asafoetida, or Devil's Dung, the traditional banishment herb to remove demons.

Banishment Incense
1 Part Dragon's Blood resin
1 Part Black Copal
1 Part Frankincense
2 Parts Patchouli Leaves
1/8 Part Garlic Powder

While not the most pleasant smelling of incenses, it does cast out and put up a wall against harmful forces and energies.

While Dragon's Blood is used to banish spirits, it can also be used to call spirits, as in this incense formula.

Spirit Calling Incense
3 Parts Myrrh
2 Parts Dragon's Blood resin
1 Parts Black Copal
2 Parts Rose Petals

2 Parts Mugwort
1 Part Star Anise
1 Part Wormwood
1 Part Eyebright
1/2 Part Elder Flower
1/2 Part Datura Leaf
1 Pinch Nutmeg
10 Parts Warm Red Wine

Powder and mix the dry parts, and then add the wine to bind them together. Let it dry and break into smaller pieces.

Lastly, Dragon's Blood can be used to call the spirit of the Dragon. Dragon mythology is varied, to say the least. Modern ideas of dragons range from powerful astral entities, embodiments of kundalini energy and chthonic forces linked to lay lines. Particularly, the images of the red and white dragon of the land show up in Welsh mythology and the stories of Merlin. Here is an incense to help attune to the dragon power of the land.

Red Dragon Incense
3 Parts Red Sandalwood
2 Parts Dragon's Blood resin
1 Part Myrrh
½ Part Tobacco
½ Part Wormwood
¼ Part Tarragon
¼ Part Hawthorne Berries
¼ Part Rose Petals
5 Parts Red Wine
1 Part Honey

Mix the dry ingredients together and use the honey and wine to bind them. Let the mixture dry and break pieces to burn upon charcoal to summon the dragon power. Best done outdoors. Those seeking a White Dragon formula could try formulas of White Sandalwood, White Copal, Mugwort, Jasmine, Camphor, Mistletoe, and Datura, making a more lunar or stellar oriented dragon incense.

While Dragon's Blood can be added to water based potions, it will sink to the bottom of the vial. It is best used in high grade alcohol potions, tinctured, as the alcohol will better dissolve it, making a stain. A simple but effective power potion of Dragon's Blood would be:

Dragon Power Potion
4 Cups Grain Alcohol
1 Tablespoon of Dragon's Blood (powdered resin)
1 Tablespoon of Rose Petals
1 Teaspoon of Cinquefoil Leaf
½ Teaspoon of Oak Bark
1 Pinch of Tobacco

Mix together on the first Tuesday after the new Moon, and let it sit in the dark for about six weeks, straining and bottling on the second full Moon, when the Moon is still waxing in light. Put a drop or two on spell papers and talismans, wear upon the wrists (it will leave a stain) or use it to consecrate other tools and objects. It can be used for any purpose.

Dragon's Blood is famously used in Dragon's Blood Ink, to write spells and create paper talismans, though the ink can also be used like a "paint" to mark ritual objects relating to fire and Mars. It makes an excellent stain for wooden wands. Most commercial Dragon's Blood Ink mass produced is simply red ink or dye with a label marked Dragon's Blood. A more magickally potent formula for Dragon's Blood ink is simply a tincture of powdered Dragon's Blood resin in high grade grain alcohol, thickened with gum arabic. Some will add the ashes of oak to thicken it as well. It forms a base for many other magickal inks, with other oils and resins added to it. I like to add a little frankincense resin or oil to it, to bring solar fire along with the Mars energy. Dragon's Blood ink can also be used to seal a spiritual pact, between people, or between humans and spirits.

Love Charm
1 Teaspoon of Dragon's Blood resin
1 Teaspoon of Rose Petals
1 Teaspoon of Damiana
1 Teaspoon of Vervain
1 Rose Quartz

Here is a simple love charm to be made on a Friday when the Moon is waxing. Mix the herbs together for love and sexuality, and place a blessed rose quartz in the mix. Gather them all together in a red or pink bag, and carry it on your receptive side (left side if you are right handed, right side if you are left handed) to attract a lover.

Baths are an excellent way to cleanse and remove harmful energy, particularly when we feel we have been cursed or "crossed." This powerful uncrossing formula comes in the form of a bath salt. It can be made and stored for when you need it.

Dragon's Blood Bath Salts
Dragon's Blood and Frankincense Tincture
1 Cup of Sea Salt
7 Drops of Hyssop Essential Oil
7 Drops of Lavender Essential Oil
3 Drops of Lemon Essential Oil

Dissolve the resins of Frankincense and Dragon's Blood in grain alcohol. I suggest 4 Cups to one Tablespoon of each powdered resin. Let it steep for at least four weeks. Pour the liquid over the salt, just enough to dissolve the salt. Then leave it open and allow the alcohol to evaporate, leaving a reddish brown salt. You can enhance the salt's color with a little red food dye, but the dye and the resin may stain your tub, so be aware. Add the essential oils and mix thoroughly to the dry salt, then bottle. Use about one tablespoon in warm water and soak for at least ten minute. Let the water drain out of the tub while you are still in the tub, taking all harmful energy away, and then rinse and cleanse yourself as you would.

Dragon Tree Flower

For those wanting to work with the living plant, Dragon's Blood can be a hard one to find. For most American' Witches, it is near impossible to cultivate. I was blessed to experience a Dragon Tree, *Dracaena draco,* in the Brisbane City Botanical Gardens while on tour in Australia. Author Gede Parma took me to see it. It had a beautiful pink-magenta five petalled cup like flowers blooming and a red resin could be seen in the palm bark from a wound in the tree. It was a powerful attunement, really demonstrating to me the magickal nature of the tree, and the resin I so love to use. Even if you don't ever get to be in the physical presence of a Dragon Tree, use the resin to attune to its spirit, and find the blessing of dragon magick yourself.

Sources

Beyerl, Paul. *A Compendium of Herbal Magick.* Phoenix Publishing, Inc. Custer, Washington, 1998.

Beyerl, Paul. *The Master Book of Herbalism.* Phoenix Publishing Inc, Custer, Washington, 1984.

Cabot, Laurie with Tom Cowan. *Power of the Witch: The Earth, the Moon and the Magical Path to Enlightenment.* Dell Publishing, New York, 1989.

Cunningham, Scott. *Cunningham's Encyclopedia of Magical Herbs.* Llewellyn Publications, St. Paul, Minnesota, 1985.

http://en.wikipedia.org/wiki/Dragon's_blood

https://www.otherworld-apothecary.com/catalog/botanicals/ dragons_blood.html

The Mandrake

By Raven Grimassi

t is impossible to think of plants that are associated with Witchcraft and not have the Mandrake at the top of the list. It appears in ancient writings of the pre-Christian era and continues to be mentioned over the following centuries and up into modern times. There are four plants that are given the name "Mandrake" although only two of them are actually those of the botanical group. These are the Mandragora officinalis (or officinarum) and Mandragora autumnalis.

In Old England when the Mandrake is mentioned in magical texts, the plant is actually the white bryony (Bryonia dioica). The root and fruit of this "English Mandrake" is similar to the "official" Mandrake, which is native to southern Europe. The leaves of English Mandrake, however, are very different and resemble some forms of ivy. The root of the white bryony, like that of the Mandragora, is toxic.

The fourth plant that is the so-called American Mandrake, which is commonly known as the May Apple. Its botanical name is *Podophyllum peltatum,* and it is native to North America. The May Apple is toxic, and like the Mandrake and the white bryony, it should be used with care.

The root of the Mandrake is legendary and is often depicted in human form. Indeed many Mandrake roots are shaped like a human body, and the roots can be as large as three feet in length. They have a texture similar to a carrot, but thicker in appearance (sometimes as much as a potato at the center of the root). Folkloric references sometimes call the Mandrake "the plant that wanted to be human" or the "burrowed man" of the woods. However it should be noted that not all Mandrake roots resemble human form. In some cases, the roots can be taken from the soil, carefully carved to look human, and then be placed back into the soil. The carved areas will heal and the root will continue to grow.

Old occult tales tell of the "sorcerers' root" and refer to it as the master of all plants. This root is the Mandrake and is traditionally carried in a pouch by the person who owns it. Each full moon the root is anointed with scented oil (traditionally with Master Oil) and then left in the moonlight when the moon is directly overhead. It must be retrieved before sunrise.

In magical tradition, the Mandrake root can be bathed in fresh water. The water is then put into a special bottle that is not used to contain anything else. It is said that if a person sprinkles this water on anything it will flourish. This belief gave rise to the practice of sprinkling Mandrake water on crop fields, herd animals, and upon one's money. In occult tradition, this boon is only granted once every four years, and therefore can only be performed in accord with this cycle.

To carry a sorcerer's root is to be connected with the spirit of the Mandrake species, the collective consciousness. The old belief is that the powers of the Mandrake that lie beneath the earth can be invoked or evoked as desired. This increases the power of anyone who wields the sorcerer's root. In connection with this theme is the belief that the Mandrake root grants influence over spirits of the dead, and for this power the root must be anointed at a crossroads or in a cemetery in the dark moon.

The powerful nature of the Mandrake is in sharp contrast to the fact that the plant itself is very sensitive. Overwatering, under watering, digging the plant up, or even handing the leaves, can cause the Mandrake to sulk. In a short time, it will lose its leaves and appear to be dead. For this reason, don't despair if a Mandrake loses its leaves and they don't come back for weeks, if not months. The Mandrake may simply be biding its time.

A popular superstition connected to the Mandrake is that it "screams" when pulled from the ground, its scream said to be deadly. Old woodcut images show a dog tied to the base of the Mandrake with a rope, which is intended to pull the root out of the ground when the dog is made to run. The idea here is that the dog dies in place of the human who desires the root. In the mystical tradition the lore is about the spirit entity within the plant that is driven out when the plant is assaulted in this way. The "scream" is the energy disturbance, which can be problematic for the person claiming the plant.

During the Christian era, the demonization of pagan spirits and deities resulted in the depiction of the Mandrake spirit as something diabolical. The Mandrake begins to lose its mystical connection with secret places in the woods where magic users go to collect herbs. Gradually the lore turns to finding a Mandrake beneath or near the place where a criminal was hung for his crimes. Odd ideas then form around this new lore, and we find mention that the Mandrake springs forth from the urination of the hanged man upon the ground. This is a morphing of an earlier belief that the Mandrake grows from semen spilled on the soil, and it takes on the form of a human as the result of this act.

In old witch lore, the Mandrake is taken from the soil in a special manner. The person is to face west and then trace three concentric circles around the plant. Returning to face west, the person then pours a potion made of milk and soothing herbs around the base of the Mandrake. The plant is then told why it is needed, permission to take some rooted is asked, and then the soil is removed on one side of the Mandrake, exposing its roots. Using a sharp knife, a piece of root is quickly removed. The soil is then placed back to fill the hole.

In some occult traditions, the Mandrake is called Circaeon, which identifies it with the sorceress of ancient legend named Circe. In this regard, we can think of the Mandrake as Circe's root (or plant). However, a longstanding tradition places the Mandrake under the dominion of the goddess Hecate. She is often connected to the crossroads, a place in ancient beliefs where the dead gathered and where witches came to practice their ways.

The ancient writer Ovid provides a classic evocation used by the witch known as Medea. This timeless enchantment can be used before taking a Mandrake plant or prior to working magic with one:

"Diana, who commands silence when secret mysteries are performed, I invoke you.
Night, faithful keeper of my secrets, and stars who, together with the moon, follow on from the fires of the daylight, I invoke you.
Hecate of the three faces, who knows all my designs, and comes to help the incantations and the craft of the witches, I invoke you.
Earth, who furnishes witches with powerful herbs, and you Breezes, Winds, Mountains, Rivers, and Lakes, and all the gods of the groves and all the gods of the night, be present to help me.
Proserpina, night-wandering queen, I invoke you.
Hecate, Diana, Proserpina, look kindly now upon this undertaking."

Mandrake

Poke

By Michael Lloyd

Poke

Phytolacca americana, Phytolacca decandra
Other names: branching grape, cocan, coakum, crowberry,
garget, inkberry, pigeon berry, pocan, pokeberry, poke root,
pokeweed, scoke, Raisin d'Amerique.
Planet: Saturn
Parts Used: Dried root, tender shoots, berries
Magickal properties: Uncrossing, hex breaking (dried root)
Medicinal properties: emetic, purgative, narcotic (POISON)
Other uses: food (tender shoots), ink (berries)

Description

   Poke is a perennial bush that grows up from a single large
tap root. Although it dies back each fall, particularly in the
north, the bush can achieve up to 9 or 10 feet in height during a
growing season with a spread of 4 to 6 feet. Poke is indigenous
to North America, but has been spread by man to Europe and
parts of Africa and Asia. One or more greenish to wine-red
hollow stems will sprout from a single tap root, and each can
reach up to 3 inches in diameter at the base in older plants. The
tap root, which is the part of the plant with the greatest
interest to the magickal practitioner, continually grows
throughout the life of the plant and can attain the size of an
adult man's thigh in older plants (forearm-sized roots are not
unusual in plants a few years old). Poke thrives in deep, rich,
moist soil, but it can be grown under many conditions and is
particularly prolific in disturbed soils. Poke is a jealous
occupant of the garden, and will tend to shade out and
eventually crowd out any shorter competition or companions.
Poke berries are purple-black in color and hang in a cascading
bunch from a single main stem (Asian poke, var. esculenta, has

upright fruiting stems). Birds find these berries a very attractive food source from late summer to early fall, as any automobile owner who lives within close proximity to the plants can attest. With its size, reddish stems and drooping bunches of fruits, poke is a handsome and dramatic ornamental plant. The seed is readily spread by birds, to the point where the plant can become a nuisance weed to the herb gardener willing to devote the space to grow it. The berries will easily stain clothing and skin when ripe and with but the slightest touch, and so cultivation next to pathways and sidewalks is not recommended.

Magickal Uses

Poke is considered by most practitioners to be a plant of Saturn and, as such, can be used like Kronos' scythe to sever the connection between its user and the spellwork of others. This explains why the main magickal use of poke root is uncrossing hexes and breaking black curses placed on the practitioner by his or her enemies. The powdered root can be spread around the outside of the home or on the perimeter of the property to confuse one's adversaries and counter negative magick directed at the inhabitants from without. This use is also said to be effective against the actions of troublesome or hostile neighbors. Some practitioners advocate creating an infusion of poke root in uncrossing oil and applying this to the body, while others suggest mixing powdered poke root in bath water. Given the concerns over toxic mitogenic compounds in the root (see "Medicinal uses"), methods that result in direct skin exposure are not recommended. Carrying the dried root is believed by some to confer the same level of protection to an individual.

Poke has been identified by some herbalists as a visionary herb. There is some historical evidence to support this application, particularly in attempts to see and contact spirits. However, the dosage level at which the narcotic effects of

North American poke are expressed are said to be greater than or equivalent to the level at which toxicity occurs. Therefore, poke cannot be said to be safely used for this purpose. Poke root has been used as a substitute for Mandrake (*Mandragora officinarum*) in ritual, especially in the construction of poppets when Mandrake root is not available for this purpose. A bifurcated root is more efficacious for this application. Poke root is sometimes used by dishonest vendors to adulterate dried Mandrake and belladonna (Atropa belladonna) root.

Medicinal Uses

At one time Poke was a medicinal herb commonly used by indigenous peoples and early settlers of North America. The Pamunky tribe of Virginia, for example, made a tea of boiled poke berries to treat chronic rheumatism. Poke could be found in the American pharmacopoeia until the early 1900s, and was primarily used internally as an emetic and purgative, and externally to treat a variety of skin conditions. It has also been investigated for use in treating certain types of cancer. Poke contains a number of toxic compounds – resinoid phytolaccin and phytolaccic acid, saponin glycosides, and unidentified components with mitogenic (cell-altering) properties. While the toxins are at their highest concentrations in the root and the seeds, all parts of the plant are now considered poisonous and should not be ingested. Because of concerns over the mitogenic components and their potential to adversely affect blood cells, there is also some concern about absorption of active principles through the bare skin. It is therefore recommended that fresh plant parts be handled with gloves, and that powdering activities with the dried root be conducted outside or in a well-ventilated area. Avoid breathing the powder and dust. It is recommended that powdering tools (e.g., herb and nut grinders, mortar and pestle) used for grinding dried poke root not be used afterwards for foodstuffs. Children and even adults are sometimes poisoned by ingesting the attractive berries, but their inherent bitterness generally tends to limit this problem.

Other Uses

Despite toxicity concerns, the sprouts of the plant are often used in "poke salad," particularly in the south where it is considered a spring tonic and blood cleanser. The tender shoots are harvested before the appearance of red coloring in the stems. After soaking in salt water, the shoots are boiled at least two or three times, with a rinsing and water change between boils. Even after these precautions, many medical experts believe that the phytolaccatoxins are not sufficiently deactivated by this process and so caution against human consumption.

The berries produce a bright purple juice. Poke berry juice was used as an ink substitute by Confederate soldiers during the Civil War, and a number of examples of this use survive in historical archives. This juice can likewise be used in magickal journals and for writing spell scrips. Although the juice is a deep purple, ink made from the juice will be brown in color when dry. The ink can be made by expressing fresh berries or frozen berries upon thawing. If the juice is to be kept for longer than immediate use, it is suggested that vinegar or sulfur be added as a preservative. However, the latter additive in particular will adversely affect the long-term stability of the paper on which it is used.

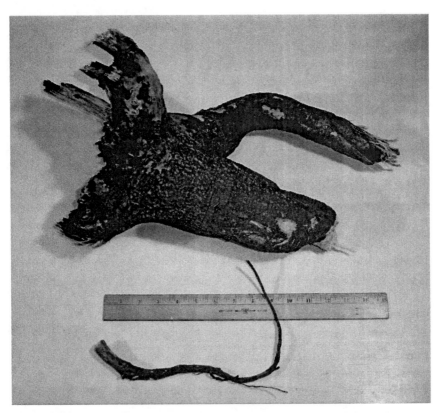

Poke Root: Fresh poke root (top) from a 7-year-old plant. Although bifurcated, the large size of this root makes it less useful for poppet construction. Dried poke root (bottom) from a 1-year-old plant. (photograph courtesy Michael Lloyd)

Sources

Beryl, Paul. *A Compendium of Herbal Magick.* Custer: Phoenix Publishing. 1998.

—. *The Master Book of Herbalism.* Custer: Phoenix Publishing. 1984.

Cunningham, Scott. *Cunningham's Encyclopedia of Magical Herbs.* St. Paul: Llewellyn Publications. 1995.

Grieve, Mrs. M. *A Modern Herbal.* New York: Dorset Press. 1994.

Hutchens, Alma R. *Indian Herbology of North America.* Boston: Shambala. 1991

Kingsbury, John M. *Deadly Harvest: A Guide to Common Poisonous Plants.* New York: Holt, Rinehart and Winston. 1972.

Lewis, Walter H. and Memory P.F. Elvin-Lewis. *Medical Botany: Plants Affecting Man's Health.* New York: John Wiley & Sons. 1977.

Rätsch, Christian. *The Encyclopedia of Psychoactive Plants: Ethnopharmacology and its Applications.* Rochester: Park Street Press. 1998.

Roséan, Lexa. *The Encyclopedia of Magickal Ingredients: A Wiccan Guide to Spellcasting.* New York: Paraview Pocket Books. 2005.

Yronwode, Catherine. *Hoodoo Herb and Root Magic: A Materia Magica of African-American Conjure.* Forestville: Lucky Mojo Curio Company. 2007.

Poppy
By Kenaz Filan

any contemporary sources would have you believe the spirit world is entirely a benevolent place where wise allies wait to dispense wisdom and unconditional love. Before we buy into this scenario, we might do well to meditate on the Hermetic axiom, "as above, so below." In our material realm, those who offer assistance generally expect payment for services rendered. A few may act out of love, pity, or a sense of duty, but most are motivated by self-interest, enlightened and otherwise. To better understand this, consider one of our most powerful and controversial plant allies – *Papaver somniferum,* better known as the Opium Poppy.

The Beginning

Some 7,500 years ago, farming communities began to develop along the banks of the Danube; within two hundred years, agriculture could be found in an area stretching from northern France to Ukraine. They used seeds and technology which had originated in modern-day Turkey, Syria, Israel, and Iran, planting peas, lentils, and other non-native crops. But they also grew another crop which originated not in the east but along Europe's Mediterranean coast – Poppies. From their original home in Spain, Poppies were carried through Central Europe; their first step in a journey which would take them around the world.

At this time, agriculture involved laborious, backbreaking work. Forests were cleared with fire and flint tools. Sticks were used to till the earth and dig roots out of the ground. Poppy seeds are edible, but lentils and wheat were much more efficient sources of food. Poppies provide oil, but so did animal fat from abundant game. Cattle will eat bitter-tasting poppies only if no other food is available – and they run the risk of intoxication and even death if they consume too much. But despite all this, Neolithic farmers dedicated a great deal of effort to growing this crop. At Egolzwil, a site dating back over 6,000 years, Poppies were the most common crop, more common than wheat, barley, or flax. Today Poppies are grown on every continent save Antarctica. But how did this flower endear itself so strongly to us? What inspired us to enter into a symbiotic (if sometimes contentious) relationship with this humble plant?

When damaged, P. somniferum produces a bitter, sticky latex containing over fifty alkaloids. The most notable of these, morphine, mimics the brain's endorphins, chemicals which reduce pain, cause drowsiness, and produce feelings of euphoria. Poppy latex (better known as opium) can contain between 8% and 25% morphine. Those who consume it experience analgesia, relaxation and, in sufficient quantities, hypnagogic visions. An archaeological dig at Crete revealed a "Poppy goddess" idol: she wears a necklace of Poppy pods and stares out at the world with a blissful sleepy-eyed smile. In Sumeria a tablet from the fourth millennium BCE describes old women and children scraping Poppy pods and collecting the juice. In Egypt an angry Sekhmet was pacified with a vat of Poppy beer, while the Ebers papyrus, a 15th century BCE medical scroll, prescribes opium as a remedy to pacify crying children.

While many other plant allies have faded from public view, Poppy still commands a loyal following of visionaries. In 19th century France, Charles Baudelaire sang opium's praises. In the 20th century, an institutionalized Antonin Artaud wrote paeans in praise of his beloved morphine. Fifty years before Seattle's grunge rockers, jazz musicians bonded over the needle. As Red Rodney, a trumpeter who played with Charlie Parker, said: "[heroin] was the thing that gave us membership in a unique club, and for that we gave up everything in the world. Every ambition. Every desire. Everything." Nor is addiction confined to the decadent West. An estimated 2.8% of Iran's population – some four million people – are addicted to heroin or opium.

But Poppy is important not only to artists and mystics, but to medical professionals as well. Today morphine remains the gold standard for pain relief. Most modern painkillers are directly or indirectly derived from Poppies: thebaine, another alkaloid produced by P. somniferum, is the precursor for drugs like oxycodone, oxymorphone (Opana™), hydromorphone (Dilaudid™), and hydrocodone (Vicodin™). The morphine and codeine produced by Poppies can be used to alleviate coughs. And what many modern users consider an unpleasant side effect – opiate constipation – could be a great blessing for healers faced with a cholera or dysentery outbreak. Even today some 1.5 million children die every year from diarrhea-related diseases. Indeed, it has so many potential uses that doctors in 19th century America referred to morphine as GOM – "God's Own Medicine."

The Spirit Ally's Bargain

But for all the benefits she offers, Poppy can be a very harsh mistress. The euphoria she produces can become an end in itself. She will happily soothe away your cares and your worries – even if they are important cares and valid worries. In her arms, supplicants may lie in bliss while their world crumbles, forsaking everything for her delights. Should they seek their leave, they will soon discover that Poppy has an unpleasant surprise in store for them.

Opiates mimic endorphins: to compensate for their presence, the body downgrades its own production of these necessary chemicals. When the user stops taking opiates, they suffer a painful period of readjustment. Body aches, gooseflesh ("cold turkey"), restless leg syndrome ("kicking the habit"), nausea, diarrhea, and profound anxiety and dread are combined with intense craving. And when the worst of this suffering is over, the opiate addict then faces Post Addiction Withdrawal Syndrome, a period of bleak depression that can last months. All of this suffering can be "fixed" with a dose of opiates. The positive reinforcement of euphoria combined with the negative reinforcement of dope-sickness makes it very difficult for a habituated user to just say no.

Numerous governments have made efforts to rescue their subjects from Poppy's clutches. In 1839 Lin Tse-Hsü, a Chinese cabinet official destroyed over 20,000 chests of British opium in an effort to stem the rising tide of addiction among his countrymen. (In response the British Navy sent in several gunboats to protect the rights of free trade. Lin was reassigned to a remote northwestern province and Great Britain gained control of Hong Kong in the "Opium Wars.") In America, 1922's Jones-Miller Act provided for a fine of up to $5,000 or up to ten years incarceration for anyone importing, concealing, buying, selling, or assisting in the sale of narcotics. In 1973, New York's "Rockefeller Laws" made the distribution of heroin a felony equal to first or second degree murder.

But Poppy is a skilled seductress, capable of ensnaring her enemies as well as her lovers. Soldiers and police officers who sought to enforce the law ran headlong into the inexorable Law of Supply and Demand. Banished from polite society, Poppy and her potions found a welcoming audience on the black market. When opiates were outlawed, only outlaws could sell opiates – and they did so gladly when they realized the potential profits. And the wages to be made as an honest lawman pale beside the potential payoffs to customs officers and cops who are willing to look the other way or assist the trade. Half of all police officers convicted as a result of FBI-led corruption cases between 1993 and 1997 were convicted for drug-related offenses. A 1998 report by the General Accounting Office cited drug-related police corruption in Atlanta, Chicago, Cleveland,

Detroit, Los Angeles, Miami, New Orleans, New York, Philadelphia, Savannah, and Washington, DC.

Poppy's influence goes far beyond precinct houses and drug dens. She helps fund organizations like the Taliban (who earn an estimated $300 million a year from Afghanistan's opium trade) and various Mexican narco-gangs who have flooded the western United States with "black tar heroin." And while the U.S. government has been among the most vocal proponents of the "War on Drugs," they have frequently made their own deals with Poppy. In exchange for the Corsican Mafia's assistance in breaking communist-led strikes on the docks of postwar France, they allowed the infamous "French Connection" to ship large quantities of heroin into the United States. Twenty years later they would make deals with Laotian opium lords in exchange for their assistance during the Vietnam conflict.

Lessons for Magicians

Modern shamans draw their plant allies from the far-flung corners of the world. Hallucinogenic toad skins from the Amazon, intoxicating mint from the Turkmenstan desert, psychedelic bark from the African rain forest – the list of strange and exotic "ethnobotanicals" available to the psychonaut is large and ever growing. Yet historically, shamans relied upon allies they could find in their immediate vicinity and which played an important role in the lives of their tribe. Ayahuasca is less relevant to our culture than Prozac™ or Ritalin™, but few modern shamans care to explore the magic of antidepressants or ADD medication. Before we study the magic of others, perhaps we should spend some time exploring the magic in our own backyard.

We should also reconsider the idea that chemical compounds are inherently less healthy, or at best less spiritual, than plants or other "natural" substances. An entire magical discipline, alchemy, treats chemicals as living spiritual entities.

We might do well to take it seriously considering that alchemists like John Dee and Isaac Newton did. And while the plant world has provided us with many benefits, it also has its share of toxins: tonka beans, hemlock and oleander come to mind immediately.

Many psychonauts wish to draw clear boundaries between their visionary adventures and mere recreational drug usage. By separating themselves from "junkies" and "stoners", they hope to make their pursuits respectable and avoid criminal liability. But they are also buying into the Puritan idea that pleasure is corrosive and those who seek it immoral. And in privileging psychedelics over other consciousness-altering substances, they may overlook many important allies and misread many historical accounts. (Perhaps the best example of this comes from the various attempts to determine the makeup of the Vedic beverage "soma." Various hallucinogens have been presented as the active ingredient. Yet contemporary Zoroastrians in India know very well what goes into Soma – a plant which they call Haoma and which we call Ma Huang or Ephedra).

Perhaps the most important lesson we can glean from Poppy is that Robert A. Heinlein was right, there ain't no such thing as a free lunch. Poppy offers its rewards gladly. It is easy to cultivate and its magical chemicals can be extracted with little effort using rudimentary technology. In return she demands only that we support her children. Her morphine-filled pods have grown so large and thick that they will not break on their own, leaving her unable to self-seed. She has hitched her star to our wagon and become dependent on us for her continued existence – but she has also taken steps to ensure that we remain dependent upon her. Those who take her for granted will soon feel the claws which are hidden in her warm fuzzy blanket. It is a lesson to remember when approaching her or any other spirit ally. You may think of that plant as a tool for your usage. Be advised that the plant may feel the same way about you.

Wormwood, the Spirit Seeker

By David Salisbury

ost magickal traditions incorporate work with spirit allies as part of their foundational practice. Spirit allies being any type of etheric otherworld being who a magick worker can form a constructive positive relationship with. Why is it important to build these bonds? The easiest answer is that we can all use more friends. If our work is to be the most effective it can be, it's good to have some help from the other side. Spirit allies teach us about what it means to have balance in the worlds of spirit and form. They teach us the ways in which energy moves and shapes us. In return, their service to us helps them fulfill their own personal work they need to do in their world to move on to something more.

The best way to build relationships with a spirit ally, be it an ancestor, angel, or some type of elemental spirit, is to simply engage in constant regular contact. Most practitioners employ some type of journey work or visual meditation to achieve first contact and the continual communications that follow. The tools we use for these contact journeys can be important, shaping the way we approach the spirit allies and how our relationships form with them. Plant magick is my favorite method for working with spirits and guides. The reason being, every plant has its own unique spirit connected to its individual root system and its species as a whole. Because of this, when you work with plant magick for spirit connection, you're really working with two spirits. The spirit ally you're contacting, and the spirit of the plant. The plant spirit operates in much the same way that any other spirits ally would. This makes it much easier to connect with any other spirit you're trying to reach. It can be a quicker process for your plant spirit to help you establish contact with your otherworld spirit.

When it comes to working with spirits, there is perhaps no better plant to work with than Wormwood. Its name *Artemisia Absinthium*, gives us a hint to the theme of its nature. The plants association with the Roman Artemis tells of us Wormwood's lunar and ethereal qualities. Artemis races through the forest, the stag at her side. She hunts with the crescent moon as her bow, riding the mist that forms the veil between the worlds. What better energy to invoke for spirit contact than that? Other than its obvious lunar associations, Wormwood is also connected with Pluto, owing to its mysterious and somewhat misunderstood nature. Elementally, Wormwood is a fiery plant, igniting the fires of our psychic vision, to see past the world of form into the world of thought and spirit.

To use Wormwood for spirit contact, we'll mix up an incense powder to burn during a spirit ally meditation. Traditionally, Wormwood is burned with sandalwood (certain nefarious lore links this with conjuring spirits in graveyards to perform a bidding). I like to kick it up a notch by using Wormwood as a base and adding in some other herbs with similar spirit calling properties. The thistle and angelica also add a protective "higher vibration" energy to the mix that's very helpful with this type of working.

Spirit Ally Summoning Mix
3 parts Wormwood
1 part dandelion
1 part thistle
1 angelica

Cast a protective circle. For the working, enter into the deepest meditative state you can in whatever way works best for you. Begin burning the spirit mix, sprinkling more on the coals after the smoke begins to fade. Incorporate deep breath work and call upon whatever spirit guides you currently have a relationship with to help you forge contact with new ones. Feel the smoke twisting and coiling around you as you ask the plant spirits to take you deeper into the realms of your spirit allies. Keep your mind open to all possible contacts yet focused on the intent for forming new spirit relationships. If you have a type of contact in mind, feel free to reach out to that type of being now. Ask the Wormwood spirit to reach into the otherworld and grab the attention of the spirit who will best aid your practice and theirs. Take your time.

When the spirit appears to you, make friends like you would any person you'd meet. Traditional magicians would caution you at this time to challenge the spirit, asking its name three times to prove that it is who it says it is. Personally, I feel that a properly prepared circle and the protection of your guides is all you need to ensure that you're meeting the right one. Like any magickal system, use whatever method you favor along with your best judgment. The spirit you meet may have much to tell you, giving you words of advice or even a gift. It may also have not much to say at all, simply being present in the experience of getting to know you.

When your meeting is done, thank the spirit ally for its time, as well as the spirit of Wormwood and the other plants you used. You can bury the herbal remains or place them in a charm bag to carry with you through the day, reminding you of the connection you forged with a new spirit ally.

Interestingly, Wormwood also has very strong associations with love, more so than any other spirit calling herb. This to me indicates that Wormwood is a favorable plant to get to know for making contact with energies that call to the core of your heart self, your center. The process of starting new relationships with spirit allies is also the process of deepening relationships with our inner selves. The true heart of all we are and do.

Part Three:
The Trees

My Journey with the Apple Tree

By Shea Morgan

y journey with the Apple Tree has been a winding path that includes visits from Mushroom, Opossum and the Fey, with other guests sprinkled in along the way, adding more spice to Apple's message, filling in the web with their connections. It definitely takes a village of guides showing the way on a journey through a year of shamanic witchcraft, and they accompanied me, walked with me, and offered their wisdom. Apple is a gateway to wisdom, and I am just beginning to understand its gifts.

For years we have had several apple trees at our family Century Farm, which has been in our family, on my Mom's side, for over 100 years. The apple trees were planted by my parents, and Mom harvests the apples every year, making pies, baking, and sometimes canning apples. Baked apples have always been a fixture of our fall and winter meals, with a little bit of cinnamon, of course. I loved the smell of baking apples as a child, and still do.

As a witch, the Apple Tree and its fruit play a major role in our lore. The center of much of the stories, of course, is the five pointed star that you will find in the center of an apple, if you cut it horizontally. It contains the pentagram, which is used for magick of many kinds and includes the four elements, spirit, and ultimately contains the mystery.

Apples come in different colors and their species have been widely varied and new strands propagated, but when we think of the apple, we think of the juicy, red apple of our childhood and mythos. The apple can also be seen as the maiden, mother and crone. The Maiden is represented by the juicy, untouched and unblemished white flesh, the Mother by the protective red covering, and the Crone by the small, black, bitter seeds, containing some poison, yet also containing the essence for regeneration in the spring.

When you think of love, or perhaps a correspondence for a love spell, you do not necessarily think of Apple as a first choice. Rose is usually the first pick. But what of the apple? Apple is a child of Venus and has many powers, including love. Think of the scent of Apple on the spring breeze when new love is beginning to take form. Such magickal properties often show up in regular life. I am reminded of the old wives tale - turn the stem on the apple while reciting the alphabet, and you will find the initial of your love in the letter on which the stem releases from the apple. I learned this as a child, yet I must admit that to this day, every time I have an apple, you can catch me turning its stem. Apple is not just for love of course. It has properties of healing, happiness, wisdom, and the mysteries.

With apples abounding and hearing Apple in our lore for years, it still took a trip across the ocean on the Temple of Witchcraft's Glastonbury Pilgrimage in August 2011 for me to make my first real connection with the Apple Tree. Glastonbury is a place of magick, and many believe, as do I, that it is the Avalon of our myths - Avalon, the Isle of Apple Trees. We are drawn to the image of the Summerland as well, with meadows and sweet apple blossoms scenting the air. What better place to begin a relationship with the Apple Tree?

One day, after we arrived back at the Chalice Well House where we were staying in Glastonbury, I went for a walk in the gardens. It was so incredibly beautiful, and I walked without thought and let the spirits move me. First I came upon an apple that had fallen in the path, and I saved it to put on our altar. As I continued to walk, I was drawn off the path. I stumbled upon a circle of Mushrooms near an apple tree. Understanding the strong relationship of the Fey to both Mushrooms and Apples, it makes sense that in such a magickal place, where the land spirits are so active, that the three would be found together – Apple, Mushroom, and Faery.

That night, Christopher Penczak did a teaching on the Nine Morgans. Afterwards, we went out to the Chalice Well Gardens under the night sky to do a journey. We walked through the lavender that lined the path, with it brushing our robes and scenting the night air. We walked to the Apple Tree and all gathered underneath its low-hanging branches. I realized that this was the apple tree earlier in the day that had gifted me an apple for our altar. Our journey's intention was to visit the Isle of Avalon and meet one of the Morgans. Christopher started by reading this hauntingly beautiful poem that he wrote.

I was sitting cross-legged under the apple tree as he read, and there was an incredible, crazy heartbeat rushing through my body – its energy spiraling up and down my body. It was from the Apple Tree. Then Christopher guided us into a journey. I felt so close to the Apple Tree. I moved into the Apple Tree, and it became my journey vehicle as I rode its trunk down below and through the dirt, and dropped through the earth. It was my gateway to Avalon, to the Undeworld and to the land of Faery. There was a river coming from the blackness of a cave, and it was feeding the lake around the island. I walked over towards an apple tree, and one of the Morgans walked over to greet me. It was Morona, the Morgan of the Earth. She was fair skinned, had black hair and was wearing a black dress. She had me sit on a bench with her by the Apple Tree. My matron, the Morrighan, also paid a visit under that apple tree.

Apple has been known as the Tree of Knowledge, and in some religions used as a tool of fear. For some, it is the Tree of Life or their World Tree. Indeed, one can get caught up in a quest for knowledge, for knowledge's sake, but knowledge, without experience, is just knowledge. The Morgan and her Apple Trees are something much more than this. On the path of the witch, we seek the wisdom of the three worlds on our journey to heal ourselves, others, and ultimately the three worlds. Wisdom is not something you can order up on a menu, nor can you exactly go in search of it – it is what happens on your journey when you experience the mysteries.

What better gate to the mysteries than the Apple Tree. The seeds of an apple can turn into a tree not quite like the parent tree you originally planted. Its seeds of knowledge are tempered through its own experience in becoming a new, unique tree – gaining wisdom through the process, leafing out with its own striking beauty. Wisdom is gained by experiencing the mysteries and applying your knowledge to that personal experience. No one can do it for you, which is why they call it the Work. I like to think of the Great Work as using that wisdom to heal the three worlds.

Apple is a gateway to the three worlds. It holds the Mysteries. It can take us to the Underworld and the Land of Faery. The Fey hold the wisdom of the land and are able to connect with us, sharing their wisdom, through the Apple Tree. In Avalon, the Lady in White, came to share her stories with us. Is she the Spirit of the Apple Tree? Faery? Or a combination of both? Of course, in the Arthurian lore, we are reminded of Morgana. who some say is Fey, and also of the Priestesses of Avalon on the Apple Isle. I think the Lady in White, for me, is all of these things and more. She holds a key to the gate of the Mysteries, if you choose to unlock it.

As for the apple I found and placed on our altar, the next night, Christopher placed the apple into the chalice before his teaching on the Serpents – Red and White. It is interesting that there was a connection of the apple from one night to the next, as I went from a journey with the Morgans and the Isle of Avalon, to an initiatory journey with Faery Queen Aroxanna. The Apple Tree and its fruit are definitely a gateway – a gateway to wisdom, a gateway between the worlds and a conduit to connecting with the Fey.

In that journey, there was a red stream and a white stream and their waterfalls formed a pool. As I think back on this, the red and white symbolized the serpents, the red and the white also were the apple – the red skin of the apple and the juicy white center, the blood of sacrifice and the white of purification and cleansing. I was not surprised at the connection with the Fey to either the Apple Tree or to my own journey.

Tree spirits are not shy about making themselves known when they have something to teach. When I returned from Glastonbury, going back to my mundane life, yet jumping wholeheartedly into my shadow work for the end of our year of shamanic witchcraft, the Apple Tree made it clear that it was not yet done with me. But first, the Spirit of the Apple Tree had to find a way to make me listen.

In early October, I went to visit our family farm. The apples were just ripening, and not quite ripe enough to pick. My parents and I were enjoying the night air on the screened in back porch. Next thing we saw was an opossum saunter across the backyard. He headed straight for one of the apple trees, which I soon was to realize was his first choice among apple trees. He climbed up into the tree and climbed back down with an apple in his mouth. Boy wasn't that just the happiest little opossum you have ever seen! He sat right down by the trunk and used his two front paws to eat his little prize. After he was finished, he went back up in the tree for more. The only thing that scared him away for a little while was our resident owl. This scene repeated itself the next night. My parents were a little bit frustrated that the opossum might eat all their apples, but I pointed out the absolute joy and pleasure of that little creature dining on nature's finest gift.

I really had not paid much attention to the apples trees at our farm before. The opossum, so intent on eating from the fruit of the apple tree, drew my focus back to the apple tree and made me realize the need to be silent and to listen. It drew me back from my busy life. By this little creature's interaction with the Apple Tree, I saw wisdom. The opossum had the knowledge to climb the tree, the daring and the will to do it, and in watching him, I saw the wisdom in silent moments. To me, being silent is where the mystery is, and opossums are silent. He was my guide to the apple tree, causing me to pay more attention to the apple's messages and mysteries.

I do believe in offerings to the spirits of trees, plants, animals and the land, and I do it regularly. However, I had left for home before a friend made a great suggestion, which was that I should leave an apple at the base of the apple tree. My parents were still at the farm for one more night, and my Dad, used to my seemingly strange requests, granted this one and placed an apple at the base of the tree. The next day, the apple was gone.

Then the next weekend I went back to the farm by myself for my own little shamanic retreat. It also was a rite of passage of sorts for me as well, as I had never had stayed there by myself. My second night that weekend, I made my weekly offering to the Morrighan, the Fey, and Spirits of the Place. This time I poured wine at every tree in our yard in a circle around the farmhouse. I also left an apple out in offering again for the opossum and the apple tree.

I woke up in the middle of the night, went to the kitchen and looked out the back window as I like to do, with the big old elms and the apple trees in back. The apple was gone. I let my gaze wander, and there was the opossum – he had just walked away from eating his apple. As he walked around the house, I had to go back to bed, but something made me look out my bedroom window. And there, under the moonlight was the opossum, right outside my window, and he climbed up the tree next to my window – definitely a first time for everything. The energy was crackling in this connection I felt tugging at my heart, a thing of beauty and to be honored. I thanked the Apple and the Opossum and said good night.

For me, the farm is all about stillness – the mystery that is seen and found in the quiet stillness of nature. The opossum is the stillness and the mystery is seen in the apple, which we can see in any challenge or journey if we only slow down long enough to look, peel back the mystery, and savor its juices. I must add that the opossum had a banner fall harvest - by the time my parents got back up to the farm to pick the apples, the opossum had cleaned out every last one.

Of course, the nature of the gifts of life lessons on this journey is not always easy. We need something to push against or to overcome sometimes to provide strong fuel for the fire as we blaze our soul's trail. You could look at it as biting through the apple's more bitter skin to get to the sweet pleasures and meanings inside. Or, you could look at it inverted, as the world of Faery can be viewed as inverted to ours, like the bitter poison of the seeds, working out to the sweetness of the white flesh and the protection of the apple's skin.

For a few months over the waning part of this year, I had felt the pull of the Morrighan, Hecate, Cerridwen, and Baba Yaga to write a ritual. We scheduled a Dark Moon ritual with our coven, but I actually did not write the ritual until the day of the gathering when the Dark Ladies and my guides started to speak to me. Those guides included the voice of the Apple Tree. It seems highly appropriate in considering all of this now, given the connections of the Dark Goddesses to the Apple and the Underworld. Here is the alignment with the Dark Goddess and Moon that came to me that day.

Howl of the Wolf crying out warning in the darkness
Crackling of the Oak snapping above the roar of the fire
Mushrooms finding life in the crevices of the rotting wood

Naked Birch beckoning us forth with her white fingers of bone
The Dark Lady calls us through the skeletal forest
The land walks in shadows, hiding in dampness and fog
The Hunted now at rest beneath layers of decaying leaves
Crows dancing on the brittle air in a language all their own

Depths of the ocean stillness belied by the crashing waves
Pounding the shoreline, the elements converge
Edge of the deep, water meeting air, shaping the earth
Burning with fire, we walk this path between

She shines her light through her crimson eyes for those that would follow
She calls her children to her side, together, yet we walk this path alone
Courage to hear the warmth under the screech of her cry
Warmth to those brave enough to enter her cloak

We find her there, underneath the mask, if we dare to seek
Heart beating and pulsing together with our own
The Crone, the Hag, the Magick of the Underworld at her command
She holds out the Key in her rot covered hand – will we take it, she asks?

Key to unlock the secrets of the below, of the depths and of our soul. The
    secrets of the Apple and its seeds, sweet, yet poison
Datura, whispering, calls us, intoxicating scent of attraction
The Lady has her ways and wiles; her gifts are many
Who will be brave enough to take her gifts when offered?
Where shall they bring you? Her demands are simple though not easy
She asks a path of service in return. Will you accept her hand now, and
    the key that has been offered?

The ritual was moving and poignant. Just as the Apple Tree
had gifted me with its message, and guided me in writing this
ritual, the Dark Goddesses lent their support as well. The next
morning, though it was daylight, a young opossum made a visit

My Journey wih the Apple Tree

to my home in the suburbs. It was not long after this that my parents purchased an apple tree for my backyard, and it will be planted in the same area. I had asked the Spirit of the Apple Tree to let me know one night where to plant this tree, so that I would know when I woke up in the morning. It came to me in a dream visit to tell me where to plant the tree in my yard. The Apple Tree was a fitting conclusion to this first year with the Morrighan as my matron.

It is clear that Apple drew me to its mysteries, and draws other witches, for a reason, but what is it about apples that draw everyone to them? Apples are home. They are comfort and safety. Candles are even made with the scent of Apple. We know Apple is healing and has vitamins, but why do kids like it so much? It is again about that comfort, love and happiness, such as found in the simple pleasures of life. It is safety with the pentagram, even for those unfamiliar with its mysteries.

Apples are the four seasons. It is spring blossoms and the Faery, and summer with green apples on the tree. Fall is ripening apples, reminiscent of hayrides, wassail, and family trips to the apple orchard. What is it about the apple orchard that makes it so fun? The idea of fertility and an abundant harvest as you fill up the apple baskets. Apples signify abundance and fertility, and through that, success and good luck. They are accessible and friendly trees, with low hanging fruit that children can relate to as well. We eat apples in all sorts of forms and put the rest on the compost. Any apples remaining then rot back into the earth as fertilizer for next year's growth or start their own apple trees.

We can work with Apple through our journey of the year, just as we see its growth, decline, and renewal in the physical world. Meditate with the Apple tree, become one with the tree, see and feel what it experiences. Or call on the Spirit of the Apple Tree in journey to ask what lessons it has to teach you. The possibilities are as endless as the apples in the orchard. If you chose, pick one and taste of its fruit. The next time you walk by a display of apples, give thanks to the Apple Tree for its gift of wisdom.

Birch

By Peter J. Kwiatek

here is a beautiful lady who stands at the edge of the woods. She is an elegant presence, tall and slender, inviting you in to the forest and into new experiences. The Celts call her The Lady of the Woods. She is an intrepid settler who blazes trails and founds new communities. She promises adventure and also renewal. She is famous for her self-sacrifice and healing as well as her beauty. We call her Birch.

Wherever you find the birch tree you also find a deep and loving lore about her many attributes. Birch is one of the most sacred trees in the mythologies of the Northern Hemisphere. Frequently, birch trees are found at the edge of a forest. Because of this, the tree's white bark stands out against the greens, blacks, and browns of the deeper woods. Even the barks of black and yellow birch, with their shaggy bark or their dark striations, stand out in contrast to their surroundings. Here in northern New England, birch trees often line the sides of the roads and highways. Birch trees have long, slender, and graceful branches with leaves that tremble gently in the wind. These leaves are among the first to bud in the spring. They add color and a sense of optimism during the dull and muddy end of the winter. Birch leaves also turn a brilliant yellow during the autumn. The tree is self-pollinating, both male and female, and produces long, thin catkins later in the spring. It's easy to understand why people have always revered the birch as a singularly beautiful tree.

Birch is one of the first hardwood trees to repopulate a cleared swath of land. Most of the primal forest of the American Northeast was clear cut long ago. The land was turned over to agriculture and farming. Later, these open fields were deserted and allowed to return to forest growth. Birch is among the very first trees to re-establish themselves, setting up groves and colonies across the landscape. Later, other hardwood species came in and took over the new forest. But birch blazed the trail. As the later arriving trees began to dominate the new forest, the birch stayed mostly on the periphery. This is how she got her reputation for being a symbol of change and new beginnings.

Birch has many uses, both mundane and magical. Most species have wood with a hard, straight grain. This makes it ideal for housing lumber, furniture, and utensils. Native Americans used silver birch to make their canoes. The bark was used to make medicinal bandages as well as tinder for campfires. Birch trees have well known healing properties which makes the bark suitable for binding wounds. The peels of birch bark will ignite, even when wet. Because of its tall, straight growth, the birch tree was often used as a ceremonial Maypole. In many traditions, birch was used as the Yule log. These functions seem appropriate given The Lady's association with new beginnings, the rebirth of the God at the winter solstice and the beginning of the light half of the year at Beltane. In Scandinavia, birch branches are often used to stimulate blood flow in the sauna. The pliable end branches, often with the leaves still attached, are struck on the skin. And in former, less gentle times, prisoners were ritually flogged with birch rods because it was believed that the birch caused them to confess only the truth. This practice may have continued on the Isle of Man until only a few decades ago. Apart from all these other uses, birch is sometimes made into the sweet and tasty birch beer, a cousin of the better known root beer.

But this lady is also a self-sacrificing mother. When a birch tree dies, it hosts a number of beneficial fungi which eventually causes the fallen tree to decompose and to enrich the soil. Birch lends itself to the propagation of various important fungi including amanita muscaria which is a toxic mushroom widely distributed throughout the Northern Hemisphere and later introduced to the Southern Hemisphere. It has been used for centuries in Europe, Siberia, and North America as a psychedelic component in flying ointments and vision rituals. It is more commonly known as fly agaric possibly because it is thought to have been used in Europe as an insecticide. The chaga (*Inonotus oblquus*) fungus also grows on birch. This mushroom is considered a valuable natural aid in treating various forms of cancer. The chaga mushroom is especially popular in Russia, itself famous for its birch trees. The Soviet dissident author Alexander Solzhenitsyn credited medically supervised treatments with chaga for curing him of cancer. Today chaga is commonly available at health food stores and it is recommended for a number of immune boosting therapies. Chaga is easy to identify. It forms black 'shelves' on the bole of the tree. So if you are a proficient and experienced mushroom hunter try harvesting some of this wonderful fungus and make a healthy tea. Other important mushrooms found on birch include: Turkey Tail (*Trametes versicolor*), Reishi (*Ganoderma ludicum*), Artist's Conk (*Ganoderma applanatum*), Birch Polypore (*Piptoporus betulinus*), and Tinder Polypore (*Fomes fomentarius*). Birch is truly the quintessential loving mother. She establishes her home, fosters its growth and development, and then she gives herself up to healing the Earth and those who depend on its fruits.

There are many practical mundane uses for birch, but let's now focus on the magickal properties and uses of this tree. Birch is almost universally considered a feminine tree. She is a good source for harnessing Goddess energy. The birch tree is also allied with the element Water. Some people believe birch is associated with the Sun and Venus. Others believe she is more closely related to the Moon. Why not experiment and see which correspondences work for you? Be sure to note the details of your rituals and their results in your Book of Shadows or journal. See if you find any trends to indicate how birch wants to work best with you.

Birch can be used for many magical purposes. Fashioned into a wand, birch can be used to move energy in love spells as well as spells involving fertility, maternity, new beginnings, and protection. The birch wand is effective in cleansing rituals.

Birch is traditionally used to make old-fashioned brooms, and a ritual besom of birch makes a powerful tool indeed.

Birch bark is a great tool when used as a form of paper or parchment for writing down spells or sigils. Ideally the paper should be relatively fresh and found after it falls from the host tree. The magic may have a bit more oomph if it comes from a tree that was struck by lightning. Otherwise, as with any living plant, the Witch should ask permission of the tree before taking the bark or any other portion. Be prepared to hear "no" unless you have worked with birch as a species or with a particular tree. The spell or sigil should be inscribed on the inside of the bark. Then it can be burnt to cast the spell, or it can be kept indefinitely, as in a bottle or honey pot spell.

If you are interested in using birch in a formal ritual try supplementing its power and cooperation as a magickal ally by using birch beer in your chalice. This is especially appropriate in rituals that include children or adults who wish to avoid alcohol. Once consecrated, the birch beer is as powerful as any other liquid that is traditionally used during ritual. And, of course, if you want to go all out harnessing the power of birch, you could use a birch athame or birch-handled athame as well as birch beer in the Great Rite.

As part of your spring magical routine, try cleansing your house or apartment using fresh birch branches and leaves to asperge charged water around the various rooms and the property lines. Afterward, the branch can be hung near the door to stand guard until next year's new growth. But remember always to ask permission before cutting into a live tree.

Newborn babies were traditionally put to bed in a cradle made of birch wood. The birch wood was believed to protect the newborn from harmful energies. This is a fine old custom that modern Witches can continue in their own homes

If you are working magic with a live fire, either an indoor fireplace or an outdoor fire pit, consecrate birch scraps and chips and add them to the fire for cleansing and protection.

And if you are inclined to make your own rune staves or ogham fews, then consider making them out of birch which was traditionally used for this purpose in Scandinavia and Ireland.

For the truly adventurous, partners can try performing love, sex and fertility magic while making love in a birch grove. (Needless to say, be mindful of your privacy and respectful of others'!) In some Germanic traditions the goddess Frigga would be invoked for this purpose. These are just a few possible ways to incorporate birch into your magical practice. As with any magic, do not attempt to use birch in any manner which is uncomfortable, illegal, or otherwise unacceptable to all concerned. Common sense, respect, and a thoughtful approach are the fundamental rules of the day. But this great lady lends herself to many varied uses and I encourage you to try a few and see what works best for you. The Lady of the Woods is a great friend to have.

Elder

By Raven Kaldera

ady Ellhorn, Dame Elder, they called her once, and I call her that still – is a powerful guardian as well as a healing plant. She is the guardian of the shamanic road to the Land of the Dead, as Angelica is the guardian to the shamanic road leading to the Upper World. In the spring, she is laden with lacy blossoms reminiscent of the lace on the dress of a regal woman. In the autumn, her berries are dark as her Downward Road. When I call to my Dead, I bring a bit of Elder wrapped up in purple-black cloth – some dried blossoms, a dried leaf, a bunch of dried berries, and most important, a piece of her hollow stem. It's said that whistling through or looking through her hollow stem can help you see the road that the Dead walk on. I've tried both, and I can say that if Lady Ellhorn has decided to aid you, it is indeed true. If you work with the Dead, she is a wise guide and guardian.

Lady Ellhorn is a dignified crone; stern, wise, and a bit critical. She is willing to help with any sort of healing, as long as she is respected and given the kind of deference due to a wise elder, no pun intended. She has very little sense of humor, though, and does not like being made fun of. Be careful to ask before you pick any part of her leaves, flowers, or berries – it is a courtesy that she is used to through many centuries, and she will not appreciate you forgetting.

The Elder (*Sambucus nigra* in Europe, *Sambucus canadensis* in America) was once one of the most revered trees in Europe, and certainly she retains an enormous amount of folklore. She has many names - Ellhorn, Lady Ellhorn, Battree, Boure Tree, Eldrum, Frau Holle, Hildemoer, Hollunder, Hylder, Ruis, Old Gal, Old Lady, Pipe Tree, Sureau, Tree of Doom, Yakori Bengeskro, Ellen, Alri, Holantar, Schwarzer Holunder, Holder, Holderbusch, Holler, Hyld, Svarthyll. Her American variety tends to be a little shorter than the European version – more of a shrub than a tree – but she can be easily identified by her paired and subtly toothed leaves, her delicate lacy blossoms, and her black bunches of berries.

Elder is native to all parts of Europe, and has been a popular medicinal plant since prehistoric times. She is associated with the thirteenth and last Celtic tree month, Ruis – the time just before the Winter Solstice when the nights are long and cold, and it seems like the Sun will never come, appropriate for this Tree of the Underworld. The name Elder is cognate with Hylde or Holda, and it is associated with Frau Holde in her Germanic myth of the young girl who falls through the well into an underworld. The Elder tree was also associated just as frequently with Hel the Norse Death Goddess, or other various unspecified Queens and Kings of the Realms of the Dead. A modern horticultural variety from Germany which has dark purple leaves is named "Gerda" after the dark, reclusive Norse giantess-goddess who is the bride of Frey, the golden Norse god of agriculture.

In contrast to the earlier summer brightly fruiting trees and berries, Elderberries fruit last, in the autumn, and are purple-black. Elder wood should never be burned, as it is bad luck; in medieval days "Lady Ellhorn" was treated as a sentient being who should never be cut or burned. Woodcutters and farmers treated her as a lady, a living woman in tree form, up until the 19th century in rural England. The Danes called her Hylde-Moer, or Elder-Mother, and she appears in Hans Christian Andersen's story "The Little Elder-Tree Mother". When Christianity took over, the story was changed so that Elder was supposedly the wood of Christ's cross and thus was bad luck to burn; it seems that making sure that Lady Ellhorn was not burned was more important than the reasons why. Her wood should never be used for furniture; supposedly a child laid in a cradle of Elder wood will be pinched black and blue by invisible fingers.

If an Elder tree grows on your property, leave her be. If you must cut it to make way for a building, propitiate the tree spirit with vigor. In fact, it's better to transplant her to another location if possible. Propitiating Dame Ellhorn usually calls for a few bottles of good brandy poured out on the ground – she doesn't like cheap liquor – and being honestly abject about inconveniencing her. If you transplant her, pour the brandy into the new hole before rerooting her, and add some coins and bread as well. One friend of mine did some construction on my property and we argued about the placement of an Elder bush. I insisted that the bush stay, and be untouched; my friend agreed reluctantly but then crushed and buried the bush under falling roof debris anyway. "It's just a bush!" The construction eventually had to be finished by someone else, as my friend came down with a bout of bad depression and then a ruptured gallbladder which required surgery. Never underestimate the power of a plant spirit, especially one as ancient and powerful as Lady Ellhorn.

Elder is immensely protective and is hung over doorways and windows to protect a home from evil, snakes, and robbers. Hanging it in a barn will protect livestock. She supposedly has the power to release people from evil enchantments cast on them by sorcerers. Elder leaves or berries cast upon someone or some place are a blessing. Flutes or panpipes made of Elder will call nature spirits when played, and an Elder staff (as the plant of Hela) will allow one to see through glamour. Green Elder branches were laid in graves to protect the dead soul.

This tree was used in burial rites in many areas of northern Europe. All the way back to the earliest folkloric mentions, the Elder tree is one of the two plants (the other being Angelica) whose "tubular" nature wound them up in spells to slide through and visit the Underworld. The difference between them is that Angelica is the plant of Light, by which those shamans whose alliance is with spirits of Light may safely visit the Deathlands, retrieve things for their clients, leaving quickly and safely. Elder, on the other hand, is the Tree of the Underworld and the "tube" used by shamans whose alliances remain there; they may come and go as they please by leave of the Elder-Mother.

The Elder is also sacred to Holda, the Frau Holle of German folktales who lived down the well in the Underworld. Elder leaves are carried as a charm for her blessing, but while carrying it, one must be as the good daughter in the folktale who was willing to give aid to strangers and share food and resources with the needy. Being ungenerous and unhelpful while carrying her charm will bring down her wrath upon you.

If you want to make Lady Ellhorn's acquaintance, find an Elder tree and sit under it, and very courteously converse with her. Dame Ellhorn likes one to make some respectful conversation for a bit before asking for anything, and the first thing you should ask her for is advice. Take it graciously, and then if she seems not to dislike you, ask for her help should you wish to deal with the Dead in any way. If she agrees to protect you, understand that her price may be fairly high. If nothing else, she may want to continue giving you advice and seeing you take it ... about all sorts of things. As an ally, you can carry some bits of her blossom, leaves, fruit, and stem whenever you deal with dead human souls and she will give you good wisdom on the process.

Elder was called "the medicine chest of the country people", and every part of this small tree is useful for something. The flowers, fresh or dried in tea, are used to bring down fevers and treat coughs, colds, hay fever, influenza, pneumonia, and as a gargle for sore throats and toothache; they reduce phlegm and are one of the best sweat producers. Elder opens the lungs and helps any condition where people can't catch their breath. It is mildly sedating, and cools and purges heat. It is a good remedy for infants with breathing problems, and possibly a SIDS preventative. Elderflower water is good as an eyewash, especially during allergy season; taking Elder in early spring may reduce hay fever later. It is also a mild sedative and bathing in it before bed can reduce insomnia. The leaves are nasty tasting and as such are used as a topical skin healer for hot inflammations.

Ointment made from the flowers is used to treat burns; ointment made from the leaves treats bruises and sprains. The inner bark acts on the liver, opening its vessels, used for arthritic conditions and stubborn constipation, but causes vomiting in large doses and is a purgative in small ones. A syrup of the berries builds up the blood and helps anemia, and is regularly used to fend off flu viruses; it is a good winter cold treatment for children (and anyone else). The pith is used to purge water in cases of edema; the flowers and berries can be used for a lighter remedy in these cases. Elder treats colic and digestive cramps, as an antispasmodic. It can be summed up as acting on any problem where the "tubes" of the body are blocked and cooling air or water needs to come out of them. As a cooler and heat-dispeller, Elder's acupuncture point – the door through which her spirit best enters the body – is Triple Heater 6. Press it after ingesting her and taking her into your body.

Elderberries yield green, violet, and black dyes. Elderflower water was a classic skin toner and freckle remover for centuries. The Romans used Elderberries steeped in wine as a hair dye to darken the hair. The berries are eaten in jellies and pies, being rich in Vitamin C, and were made into tonic syrups for winter nutrition. Wine has long been made from both the berries and the flowers.

To make Green Elderleaf Ointment, which is a remedy for bruises, sprains, chilblains, and wounds, make this recipe, preferably just before Beltane: 3 parts freshly gathered Elder leaves, 4 parts pork lard, and 2 parts beef suet, both strained and white. Heat the leaves gently in the fat until the color is extracted, while saying the Elder charm below; then strain through a linen cloth and keep chilled.

For Elderberry Rob, which is a remedy for colds, coughs, and bronchitis, simmer 5 pounds of freshly crushed Elderberries with a pound of sugar until it is of the consistency of honey, or if you prefer honey, add it until it is the right moistness and thickness and then simmer, while saying (or singing, as I often do):

Ellen, Ellen, Lady Ellhorn,
Eldest moon and magic born,
Holda, heal me, Ellhorn's mistress,
May the night give way to morn.

Two tablespoons mixed with 12 ounces of hot water, nightly, will help chest congestion and fight colds. You can also make a straight-up Elderberry syrup by cooking and straining the juice first before adding the sweet preserver; a "rob" was meant to be thicker than syrup. Medicinal Elderberry syrup can be found on the market under the name of Sambucol, which is glycerine-based, but you can make your own homemade version to stash in the fridge and swig when needed to stave off incipient winter bugs.

I have spoken to and worked with numerous plant spirits (in my tradition they are referred to as "greenwights") throughout the years, but two of them have always watched over me. I call them my watch-wights, and they are Elder and Belladonna. Whenever I looked for a place to live, I'd find one or the other of them growing wild at the location that turned out to be the exact right apartment or house. While Belladonna was assigned to me by my patron Goddess, Lady Ellhorn apparently just took a liking to me. As a grandmother and wisewoman figure, she advises me – especially about my health – and nags me when necessary. She is also one of my consultants when it comes to dealing with the Dead, for instance during psychic housecleaning – clearing out haunts and getting wandering ghosts through the right doors to the right places.

As my watch-wight, she also reserves the right to advise me in stern terms when she feels that I am being unwise. I wrote this poem after one such happening. I am honored to have her wisdom and her attention on me for this lifetime. Hail to Lady Ellhorn!

Clearing the Barn

You're not supposed to be out in the Sun,
She says disapprovingly as I walk past, her leaves
Brushing my shoulder. Not on so little sleep,
Not so soon after being ill. Her white flowers are
Beginning to open, like the lace spilling
From an old woman's velvet dress.
Her emerald brooch flashes. So do her eyes.
The work must be done, I say. Two more loads,
I feel myself sicken, but what would my compatriots
Say if I said, The tree told me I had to go in.
Third load, and she loses patience. Go in, you fool,
You idiot, you know what will happen. Do you
Expect I'll give comfort once you've ignored me?
Or that you can expect it from anyone else? I'll tell
Them all of your stupidity, and they will just laugh,
No matter how much tea you drink.

A friend, busy with wheelbarrow and fork
Sees me stopped in my tracks. What's wrong?
I hesitate, weigh comfortable lies, and then decide.
Friends may come and go. A watch-wight is for life.
The tree told me to go in, I say. And turn for the door.

Hawthorn

By Christine M.

"And the leaves of the tree were for the healing of Nations"
— *Revelations*, 22:2

had been given the gift of time, though my mother had passed early in the year, my younger sister the year before, and I was out of work on an injury.

Sometimes good can come out of the bad. The spring had finally come and I was eager to begin my new adventure into a part of Witchcraft I had yet to explore- the green side. A side I had yet to learn, I had never really had much of a kinship with plants, they didn't seem to grow well for me. I always planted them in the wrong places and when I really tried, mostly they just plain didn't seem to work with me!

That first day of class, Wendy took us on a "plant walk" and we ventured into the forest walking down the path as she pointed out each plant and told us about it and the "medicine" it gave of itself. We gathered a few samples as we walked along so that we could make pressings for our "materia medica". Soon we were far down the path and she turned to us and said "we are going to take off our shoes and walk barefoot through the forest, we are going to walk in silence, single file, leaving room between us. We are going to listen to the forest and then we are going to leave the path, go into the trees, and lay down and hear what the forest has to say". I remember how cold the earth was beneath my feet and how little knowledge I had of the plants around me, but I was awestruck and excited about this new adventure.

As we sat, we looked around at the plants just coming up out of the ground as they woke from their winters rest. After we had done this, we talked about what we felt and heard, and then we continued our walk, circling around and coming back up the opposite side of the forest. And just as we were about to come out of the woods, she showed it to us- a small Hawthorn with a piece of plastic tied to one branch. This tiny Hawthorn didn't even have any leaves on it yet so we couldn't take a sample for our pressing.

The summer wore on and we all became engrossed in the collecting, pressing, medicine making, and all things plant related. I even showed up for plant walks on my off time, as I wanted to learn as much as I could and felt a calling to this place called Misty Meadows. What was it about this forest that called to me? As a child my sister and I played in the forest amidst the trees and sat for hours on the moss covered forest floor. We played games pretending to be fairy-folk. Oh how I missed those days and the innocence of child's play!

But this was different, here I could actually feel the life of the forest, as it turned greener and the plants seemed to one day just suddenly appear as if from nowhere! One day I ventured into the forest alone to collect some pressings, I called out to the Hawthorn as I felt it must have leaves by now! I walked and I walked and I called and I called but nowhere could I find the Hawthorn! It must be here! She showed it to us and I saw it with my own eyes! But no, it was nowhere to be found! So I left.

The summer kept us busy with apprentice hours, collecting pressings and adding cards and information on each plant, as well as, homework assignments and experimenting with creams and lotions made with plant material. I had found that just across the street from where I live, close to the new high school, there seemed to be an abundance of plants that I needed for my collection. However, the Hawthorn eluded me. I even found a great "jack-in-the-pulpit" and even though it wasn't on our list, I photographed it and put it on the website to share with my classmates.

September came and we had one class left before graduation and I still hadn't found the Hawthorn for my pressing. We gathered for our last "plant walk" and headed into the forest. Once again we looked around to see how much the plants had changed since the first time we had walked in the forest. And Wendy turned to us and said "Now we are going to do the same walk that we did in the spring and see what is different" so off came our shoes and single file we went in silence. But this time the earth was warm beneath my feet, and it felt different than it had in the spring, almost familiar, like we had come to know each other through all the walks I had taken there. When we ventured off the path and lay on the forest floor this time, we couldn't see each other! The ferns had grown tall and green and we were lost amidst them! It was such a euphoric experience to be beneath them! Not a single bug had bothered us, as Wendy had told the forest we were coming and had asked them not to! And we all felt a new kinship with the forest. As we headed out of the forest, we talked and laughed about all that we had learned about ourselves and our newfound friendship with the forest. And as I walked, I looked at the path ahead, and as I looked down I saw something—it was a large red berry! I thought— it couldn't be! And just as I thought this, I heard "look up". As I did this, towering over my head was a large Hawthorn! I was blown away! I said "Look, Wendy, a Hawthorn"! And she said "Yes, it is!" And you know what? She hadn't even known about this tree! This tree had presented itself to me, just when I had stopped looking! It was loaded with berries and it was magnificent! It was the best day. I realized that if you still your mind and allow these green allies to come to you, they will present themselves to you! So begins my true kinship with the plant spirits...!

Learning to Listen to Trees: My Messages from Maple

By Bob Hackett

y own personal connections and lessons from Maple have been ones of celebration, transformation, and finding beauty in and through healing. Maple has always been one of my favorite Trees and one of my favored woods to work with.

Here in Maine, we get to see many of the blessings that Maple has to offer. We get maple syrup and maple sugar which keeps many of the local residents out in the forests during some of the best times of year, tapping and collecting the sap that rises and then bringing it to the "sugar shacks" to boil it down over wood fires. There is even a statewide weekend celebration where those who make Maple syrup open their operations up to visitors and hand out free samples by way of early snow cones made from snow covered with the sweet syrup they produce. I'm told it takes 40 gallons of sap to make one gallon of premium maple syrup and the trees are happy to give up their sap to the folks who have been doing this for generations. To think that the same trees have been working with these same families, in the same ways, for generations, in order to bring a unique sweetness into other lives throughout the world. This is but one of the magickal ways Maple works with us in this world.

Another bit of transition magick that Maple does, is every fall, around Samhain, Maple puts on a show that makes all the other Trees wish they were Maple. Maple trees throughout New England put on their finest outfits and "set the woods on fire" with their incredible shows of color. Many times, a single tree will have three or more different colors in it ranging from green to red to yellow and all the shades of color that fall in between. I know of no other tree that is so diverse and spectacular, foliage wise, and holds their color for so long as the Maple family. "Leaf Peepers" and photographers come from all over the world to see the fall foliage of New England in autumn and with good reason. Maple plays the starring role in this Fall celebration, and it's easy to see why this tree has connections to both the element of Fire (it shows it off in its leaves), and the Goddess Cerridwen, who rules over wisdom, transformation, passion, life, and death. Maple also has ties to the Greek Goddess Athena and the Roman Goddess Minerva. All three speak of the female aspect of Spirit, free and independent of the male. Maple is truly one of the artists of the New England forest and has an unequaled flair for color. Along with this flourish of passion, before settling into the dormancy and introspection of Winter, I can feel the Maples are a comfort to the rest of the forest. They help to calm the always alert Quaking Aspen or "Popple" as it's known up here. Maple also talks to Oak and convinces him to drop his acorns. Maple reminds him he must remember to give up his leaves before the heavy snows come or his more brittle branches will snap under the extra stress and weight. Maple is a patroness of the forest and while Birch may be the "Lady of the woods" Maple's longer life and caring nature make her a Queen in all three aspects, and she plays an important part in turning the Wheel of the Year.

Many of the local graveyards up here are bordered by large old sugar Maples and I feel they watch over our ancestors in much the same way that the Yew trees do in Europe. Maples stand ready to help those who have transitioned into the next life as well as those who are left behind. They feel the grief of those standing at the graveside and many times will also see the great-grandchildren of those who are now grieving repeat this process. They act as bridges between the worlds and witness the passion of the assembled families as they sort through their feelings for the recently departed. Then they see who returns in the years that follow to remember and speak with the departed spirits. Maple collects these passionate feelings and then pours them into Cerridwen's cauldron to be reborn and celebrated each year in this tree's spectacular displays of color and her offerings of sweetness.

I think it's most fitting that Maple's sweetness many times contributes to things made in the kitchen. The kitchen is the heart of the family and where the family most often congregates and works together toward the common goal of feeding both the body and the soul. Many times this happens directly after one of those graveside ceremonies. The ironic lesson in this aspect of Maple, that it is capable of taking something as bitter as grief and turn it into something so sweet that can be included as one of the ingredients of the food that helps ground and sustain the friends and family at the wake.

Maple also has a unique capacity for hidden beauty. Some of the most highly sought figures in wood comes from Maple. Things like burls, curly, and bird's eye figure appear in abundance and regularity in Maple like they do in few other species of trees. I find that whenever a Maple tree is wounded or damaged, it responds by healing quickly and most often the healing process brings not disfiguring scars, but delightfully useful and sometimes extravagant figures at the site of the wounding. Maples also put out figured wood at all their transition points such as the buttresses, where roots meet the trunk, or at the forks, where the main branches leave the trunk. Many times the entire trunk of the tree will be inundated with spectacular figures and we get names like tiger maple, fiddle back, bee's wing, blister maple, feather figure, curly, burly, quilted, and other descriptive terms for the different grain in maple. Even in death, maple exceeds nearly all other trees in its ability to bring beauty to transition. Cabinet makers seek out the decaying wood of sugar or hard maple (called Rock Maple up here) because of its incredible coloring and the black lines that run thru it. This type of wood is called spalted maple and those colors and lines are the signatures of different colonies of fungal decay trying to break down the dead wood. Even when the Green Devil has claimed the Maple, it retains its strength and beauty long after other trees have given in to death and begun their final contribution to their life cycles as rotting hulks or compost on the forest floor. Only Apple rivals Maple's ability to hold on to life for so long. I have seen these two types of trees that are still alive and putting out new growth even when most of the trunk has gone to rot and there's more dead tree there than there is live. A large percentage of the completely hollow trees up here are Maple and Apple, and they are finally taken by death only after they have put out too much growth to be supported by the shell that the trunk has now become. The winter winds and snow cause them to collapse under their own weight. Even then, they will send up saplings from the stumps that remain. It's as though their spirits hold onto life more tightly than the other trees. They bring passion to all they touch and their dryads never miss a chance to celebrate any event or occurrence. Even death cannot dampen Maple's spirit.

One of my earliest memories of transition was when my father and I went to my grandfather's house after the passing of my grandparents. The house had been sold and we were there to dig up one of the seedlings from a Red Maple in the front yard. My father explained that he had helped plant this tree from a seedling that came from his grandfather's house when his own father (my grandfather) bought the house that he and his brother grew up in. We dug up two of the seedlings and brought one to my Uncle Bob, who planted it in his yard, and my father and I planted ours next to our home on Elm Street. When my father moved from New Jersey to Maine, he brought two seedlings from that same Red Maple with him and planted them in the yard of the home he built with the help of his sons here in Maine. One of those trees still stands tall and beautiful in my mother's dooryard. I remember all the trials and tribulations that tree went through just to stay alive and how I labored to keep it safe from things like lawnmowers tearing up its roots or string trimmers and dog chains ripping into the bark of its trunk. Every year I'd come and prune it of "winter kill" and branches that rubbed on each other inviting disease. I did whatever I could in order to keep it as healthy as possible and it thrived as a result. I feel that looking after that tree is like looking after and honoring my ancestors.

I can still picture how the day felt when I stood on the lawn of my grandpa's old house and helped my father dig up that seedling. I can feel my departed father's energy as he told me about the history of that tree, what it meant to our family and why we were there that day. Whenever that memory dims, I can go to that tree in my Mother's front yard and touch that tree and the spirit of that day comes flooding back through the spirit of that tree.

My mother is getting on in years now, and her health is declining. I know that soon I will have to think about going over to her house in the spring and digging up some of those seedlings. I'll be sure she's away from the house and doesn't see me doing it. I wouldn't want to upset her.

I'll ask my brothers if they are interested in planting one of those seedlings in their yards. If not, I'll plant more of them in mine. I want there to be plenty of seedlings left for our children and grandchildren so they can hear Maple's messages too, especially the messages from our family that the Red Maple brings.

Oak: Door of the Forrest

By Christopher Penczak

Oak was my first tree teacher. When I got involved in Witchcraft, and the door to the world of spirits and nature opened up to me, I was so excited. I did as my teacher suggested, and went to meditate outside, to speak to the spirits of the trees and plants. I sat with my back against one of the three old oak trees in my parent's backyard, as I was still living at home. I opened my senses and began to talk to the trees, expecting a warm reception from nature. I thought I "heard" them talking amongst themselves, but not to me. I tried to join the conversation, and got no response. I started to get frustrated. I tried again. There was still no response. Wasn't nature supposed to be my friend? Hey, I'm a Witch. Look at me! Really! The Red Oak I was leaning up against, finally did respond, to my surprise, with not words, but a sense of knowing its intention. Essentially it told me, "Who do you think you are? Just because you finally can hear us and don't take us for granted doesn't mean we stop all what we are doing to pay attention to you. We move in our own time, and in our own ways, and have our own business. Our world does not revolve around humans and it's arrogant for you think it does." I'm paraphrasing in hindsight, but that was the gist of the message, and with that, I snapped out of meditation. I was shocked. All my teachers (except perhaps one) were so gentle. I had yet to receive the metaphysical bitch slap regarding my arrogance. I thought it was just enthusiasm. I was excited and wondered why the trees were not. While much modern lore paints both nature and the spirit world as eternally loving and sentimentally personal, you'll find older occult lore looks at nature and the spirit world as nature truly is, both giving and taking, but impersonal. You can find allies in these realms, but each has their own way of being. From that point on, I gave acknowledgement and respect to the three oaks on that little hill, and made my offerings there. Soon, when I was looking for a ritual staff, during a storm a large branch of that tree fell and rolled right down the hill beneath my bedroom window. I took it as a sign, and not only made a great ritual tool with it, but started meditating under the tree again, and the oak began to talk to me directly and share with me its magick.

The magick of the Oak was really emphasized by my teachers. Training in a Celtic based Witchcraft tradition, we saw the Druids, the priestly caste of the Celts, as our magickal and spiritual ancestors. The name Druid is said to be related to the Ogham word associated with the oak tree, Duir. Druids were "Men of the Oak." They kept the mysteries of the sacred trees. Despite popular misconceptions around Stonehenge and other stone sites, the Druids worshipped in groves of trees, with the Oak being the most sacred of them. Oak has been associated with Tarranis, a Gaulish god of Lightning and storms, and mistletoe, said to be the fruit of lightning or the semen of the gods. Growing upon Oak was the most prized mistletoe according to ancient writings. While technically a parasite, the Oak seems to suffer no ill harm from the mistletoe overall, and didn't seem to bother the Druids, who were far more in tune with the life of both the trees and the mistletoe than we are today. Oak is gracious of its friend, allowing it a home.

In the mythos of the dual god, divided into Oak King and Holly King, the Oak King is usually the young god of power, of the light and growing season. When properly prepared, the acorn is a food staple, giving the Oak the status of life giving god, providing food and shelter for early people. Acorns are used in magick for fertility and protection. Acorns can be ground into a meal and used like flour. Raymond Buckland recommends such flour for the baking of sabbat cakes in *Buckland's Complete Book of Witchcraft*. They can also be roasted and used as a coffee substitute. Acorns are rich in minerals and

Oak: Door of the Forest

beneficial compounds, including beta-carotene, gallic acid, pectin, quercetin, tannin, sulfur, calcium, iron, magnesium, manganese, phosphorus, potassium, selenium, zinc, B-vitamins, and vitamin C.

The Dagda and Esus are also associated with the Oak in Celtic lore, and many of the storm and lightning gods, such as Zeus, are also associate with Oak. The Green Man images are most often depicted with Oak leaf faces, as the Green man is also the growing god of the waxing year, but horned gods such as Herne are also invoked by the burning of Oak bark. Sacred need-fires are started with Oak. King Arthur's Round Table was supposedly made from a single slice of a giant Oak tree. One version of Merlin's tale has him trapped in an Oak, and Oak wands are an excellent magical tool for the Celtic Witch or Druid. Charms and tools made from Oakwood are particularly powerful. Oak makes an excellent healing wand or staff.

Oak is part of the faery triad of trees – Oak, Ash, and Thorn. Two of the most amazing English Oaks (*Quercus robur*) "survive" in Glastonbury, as the ancient Gog and Magog. They are all that remain of an ancient passageway of Oaks leading to the Tor. While I expected magnificent Oaks when visiting, they appeared almost dead, yet still exuded power. They are the Oaks of Avalon and many believe they will regenerate again and bear new life.

Gog and Magog

Oak: Door of the Forest

Oak's magickal associations are with strength and power, as well as ancient knowledge. It is known as the door of the forest, or the hinge upon which the yearly wheel turns, perhaps referencing the Oak and Holly King mythos, for it is the death of the life god that turns the wheel, while the dark gods, while waning, is as eternal as death. Oak is associated with the Roman god Janus, two faced and opening of the doorways. In the Temple of Witchcraft, we seek the Witch God as the combined Oak and Holly King, as Janus, two faced. He is the guardian of the gate of mysteries, oak leafed and stag horned. As the tree that is both the god and the sacred gathering place, the nature temple, it opens the gate to spirit and is the gate itself.

Duir of the Oak
Door of the Forrest
Knock, knock, knock come I
Will you let me in?
Will you let me pass?
I come in Love and Trust with Gifts in Hand
And seek to pass through your dark eye.
— *The Plant Spirit Familiar*

Oak is ruled by Jupiter, and in its bark the metal of Jupiter, tin, can be found. Oak is also associated with the Sun. Some divide the different species of oak, giving Red Oak (*Quercus rubra* and similar species) to Mars, White Oak (*Quercus alba*, *Quercus gambelii* and many others) to the Moon and Sun, and Black Oak (*Quercus velutina*) to Saturn, but its general nature is tall, strong, proud, a leader among trees and falls under Jupiter. Gray Oak (*Quercus grisea*) is the protective tree of the Navajos. All oaks can be used in spells for success and good fortune, protection, love, lust, luck, healing, and purification. Oak is also excellent for grounding and being centered in your body.

Carried in the pocket, Oak can bring protection and good luck. Oak tea in a warm bath is used to purify and prepare for rituals and initiation. Burning Oak bark with rue and mistletoe will banish evil energies and spirits. Lightning struck Oak is a catalyst for magick, and forms the basis for Laurie Cabot's Witch's Lightning incense and potions, along with rabbit hair, to speed up magick and summon storms.

Oak King Oil

1 Oz of Grape seed Kernel Oil
1 Pinch of Oak Bark
12 drops of Oak moss Essential Oil
10 drops of Frankincense Essential Oil
10 drops of Patchouli Essential Oil
7 drops of Vetiver Essential Oil
7 drops of drops Juniper Essential Oil
4 drops of Cinnamon Essential Oil
Acorn

Mix the oak bark into the grape seed base oil and add the essential oils by drop, swirling them in. Put the acorn in last. This is best made on a Thursday, between the Winter Solstice and Summer Solstice.

Oak King Incense

3 Tablespoons White Oak Bark
1 Tablespoon Frankincense
1 Tablespoon Cedar Bark
1 Teaspoon Cinnamon
1 Teaspoon Juniper Berries
12 Drops of Frankincense Essential Oil
7 drops of Cedar Essential Oil
4 Drops of Juniper Essential Oil
1 Teaspoon of Honey

Mix the dry powdered ingredients first, then add the oil and honey to the powder to bind. Let dry and then store in an air tight container for a month before use.

Magickal Wisdom Tea
1 Part White Oak Bark
1 Part Cinnamon
1 Part Vervain

Mix the dry herb together and take one tablespoon of herb to one cup of boiling water, and let it steep at least fifteen minutes. Add honey to taste and drink before doing any work where wisdom, insight or awareness is needed. Though it will increase the bitterness, you can add Mugwort if doing divinatory work, or garden sage if doing healing.

As a flower essence, oak grants endurance. Oak is one of the original flower remedies of Dr. Edward Bach. Oak types are always on the go, with tremendous power to lead, succeed, but often drives forward into life as a struggle to endure. Those who benefit from Oak usually do, but Oak helps them access a deep wisdom to not force a situation, but stand with it. The higher self, the lightning of the heavens, guides, rather than the personality. Rather than work in pain, seek joy in the process. Oak people are "strong as an Oak" but the medicine and magick of Oak helps them be as "wise" as an Oak as well. While oaks do not know how to "bend" in the way that willows do, they stand tall and endure. Oak helps us explore our limits and grow into new areas. It encourages rest and rejuvenation. It's an excellent remedy for recovery from long term illness or enduring stress.

Medicinally, Oak is astringent. It tightens tissues. The White Oak inner bark is used to control bleeding, internal and external, as well as diarrhea, hemorrhoids, dysentery, and womb troubles. Oak bark can act as a diuretic to increase the flow of urine and flush the kidneys. It appears to balance the function of the kidneys, spleen and liver, as most Jupiter herbs do. It's a topical antiseptic.

My own experiences with this tree teacher tend to fall more under the gateway associations. Since making friends with northeastern Red Oak, I have been blessed with the knowledge and ability to open the spirit gate for myself and others. Various psychic talents exist, and while everyone seeks clairvoyance when training in the Craft, little talked about is the ability to be an Opener, one who can hold open the gate and show the path for others, during vision work and guided meditation. Less flashy than other predictive psychic skills, is a powerful and useful technique for ritualists and teachers helping others go deeper in their experience. Many of my herbal allies are about gateways and aiding others, but Oak has been the primary "door" through which I pass, and take my students and covenmates. Sit under an oak with patience and humility, and gently knock on the door. Eventually, the door will open and the guardian will escort you across the threshold.

Sources

Cunningham, Scott. *Cunningham's Encyclopedia of Magical Herbs.* Llewellyn Publications, St. Paul, Minnesota, 1985.

Shulke, Daniel A. *Viridarium Umbris.* Xoanon Publishing. Cheshire, England: 2005.

http://www.herbalextractsplus.com/white-oak-bark.cfm

http://herb-magic.com/white-oak-bark.html

http://www.bachflower.org/oak.htm

The Majestic Pine Tree

By Angela Pote

he image of the Pine tree varies from our memories to where we live in this amazing world. My earliest memories are lying under my family's Christmas tree and watching all the lights and garland, and trying to count how many decorations were on the tree. Others may have memories of opening their door and having the beauty of this majestic tree in their backyard. There are an estimated 125 different varieties of pine trees in the world. Their height and width along with the shape of their needles will vary from species to species. However, there are a few things that are the same in all species, or at least very close. The greatest similarity is that they are all evergreens and they all produce pine cones and resin. Their bark is very similar and seems to change with age. Pines are very old and full of wisdom. The oldest recorded pines, unquestionably, are from the *Pinus longaeva* species which many live to be 4,000 years old. Here in America, there was Promethus, who at the great old estimated age of 4,862, was sadly cut down in 1964. The oldest living tree in America at this time, is Methuselah which is 4,843 years old. On average, most Pines generally have a life span between 150 to 400 years. No matter how young or old, the magick given from the Pine is truly a gift. The Pine has amazing endurance as she rises above the Earth into the mighty skies above. The White Pine grows to between 80 and 110 feet, and they can get as wide as 40 feet. Pine trees have a host of creatures that feed from them. They eat every part from the needles straight through to the inner bark. Young black bear cubs will climb large White Pines to safety when in danger. The bald eagle builds its nest in living White Pines just below the crown on a main branch. When I think of a bald eagle, I see beauty, grace, and freedom. One of the places that it chooses to build its nest are at the top of a

White pine. I think the symbolism here has a lot it can teach us. Bald eagles stay on a main branch just below the crown. Even if the top of the pine is damaged, a nest could be made there. A nest is a safe place. We should hold the space around our crown chakra as a main safe place for the beauty we are, and the beauty we see in this world. A place where grace flows from the Goddesses and Gods we serve. We should strive to have the freedom to grow into our true selves. Their age holds wisdom, not only the deep secrets of ages past, but wisdom of the land and space that they occupy. If you are able to be in the presence of this majestic tree, take time to get to know her as she is willing to speak if you are willing to listen. Sit under, next to, or place your back against the bark of the tree and meditate with the intent to talk and listen to the spirit of that pine tree. They are, in my experience, very chatty.

I have three pines in my yard and the largest and oldest is a White Pine. I look at this gentle old soul with amazement because she has taught me to see all parts of her and in doing that, I have learned so much. The Pine needles have three times the amount of Vitamin C than a lemon and can be used in teas. Since Pine is an evergreen, we have availability to it all year long. I use this tea seasonally and what I mean is that the tea I prepare and the physical and spiritual reason depends on the season. In the warmer seasons I will steep the needles in black sun tea with lemon, mint, and watermelon. This carries a huge energy boost come midday, and has a wonderful airy taste. Heat one gallon of water, and add 6 tea bags. After it comes to a boil, place 3 bundles of needles (I tie them together) in the water to steep along with the tea bags. Leave the needles in for 20-25 minutes and remove the bundles. Place your tea along with the tea bags still in the water and let it cool to room temperature. Set in the sun for 3-6 hours and remove the tea bags. Before you place it in the refrigerator, add a bundle of fresh mint, and three sliced lemons. Before you serve, cut and add cold watermelon slices.

When the pine cones start to fall, I gather some needle bundles and I will freeze them through the winter. After all, who wants to throw on the boots to go out in the snow to gather needles in winter. Two things that we try to avoid in the winter months are colds and the flu. Both affect the respiratory system. Most of us, if not all of us, have heard it said that when you get a cold you need Vitiman C, or if you take Vitiman C it will reduce your chances of becoming sick. Well, Vitamin C may not cure a cold, but some studies suggest it may help prevent more serious complications. So with needles on hand throughout the winter months, you can make what we call a heavy "C" tea, to chase a cold away! Cut one needle bundle up and place in a tea strainer along with burdock root and sweet red pepper (yes, I said pepper). You only need to slice off two pieces. You want it for the Vitamin C, and do not want a strong taste of the pepper. Okay, back to heavy "C". Add a cinnamon stick or two after you have steeped the strainer in the boiling water for 15 minutes. Now it's time to add the final ingredient. One tablespoon of concentrated frozen orange juice per cup. This tea is great for keeping colds and the flu in check and its energy will help you get moving when cabin fever sets in. The inner bark of the White pine can also be eaten, though I have not tried it yet! I hope to. In order to eat the inner bark, the tree has to be cut down and unless you have no choice I think it's better to leave a good, healthy tree alone. Native Americans would grind the bark into flour and add it to other starchy items to stretch them through winters when food was short. And now a word about the sticky sap that seems to get everywhere when you touch a broken tree branch. For the Pine, this sap acts as a coagulant. If there is a place where the bark has been damaged, the sap will cover the area and seal it so disease and harmful agents do not enter. This is a visual reminder that the fluid part of us can be used to protect us till a damaged area can heal. When we are hurt by certain situations or circumstances, or by a certain individual, we tend to think of something hard that we can sheild ourselves with. But that does not always have to be the case. When I think of the Pine's sap, I can't help but to think of our blood, the fluid part of us, of the water that flows through our bodies. Both of these remind me of my ancestors and I think of the Summerlands. When we are in a situation that we may feel has damaged us, we can call on the sap of our souls to shield us and aid us in the healing. The smell of Pine has a great calming and cleansing scent. Some of us use it in everyday products to clean our homes, but it is much more than that.

There is gypsy lore that my Gran would say: to clean the house of evil spirits (probably because evil would sometime be associated with foul smells) and if you cleaned the area with pine (an evergreen being life), that scent would chase the evil spirits away. The needles of the White Pine are burned to keep indoor places fresh and imbued with natural magicks. Great bundles of them are burned and a person who has been attacked by a curse is placed in the smoke. This gathers up the magick of the spell and sends it back upon its caster. (The smoke is said to seek them out no matter how distant they are.) Pine symbolizes immortality and represents earth. Pine cones also represent fertility. Place a fragrant pine cone in fresh water for three days. Remove the pine cone and place a few drops of the cone water on the inner parts of your wrists and it will become a reminder of our place in the circle of life. Pine needles and the cones are also used for purification, health, fortune, and prosperity. For an earthly purification bath, gather a few fallen cones, broken cones are also good for this, and pine needles. Take a medium to large white candle. Use sage oil or frankincense oil, jasmine tea or the leaves. Take the candle and place a few drops of your oil clockwise around the top of the candle, then place the cones around the candle. In a sachet place the jasmine along with any broken pieces of cone and pine needles inside and place the sachet under the running bath water. Light your candle and say:

By fire I burn all that is dross, by water I cleanse the days lost, by air I call the mighty pine to come and purify all that is mine, by earth I sit within this bath now to enjoy my rest at last.

The majestic Pine has called earth her home for thousands of years. Full of wisdom, they stand mighty and strong, watching all who pass by. With love they show us that even in the darkest, harshest nights of winter that life will prevail.

Part Four:
Wisdoms

Herb Magic and
the Doctrine of Signatures

By Alaric Albertsson

edicine has always been practiced with a variety of underlying philosophies. Today we have acupuncture and homeopathy, as well as anatomical medicine.

Each of these functions according to its own postulates, which differ from each other as much as they differ from those which have been largely abandoned, such as Hippocrates' theory of humors. One idea that has been discarded in medicine, and rightly so, is the "doctrine of signatures". This doctrine states that a plant – or a part of a plant – bears a resemblance (its signature) to the part of the human body it has the power to heal. Thus a plant with yellow flowers was believed to be useful for urinary disorders. A plant with heart shaped leaves could help cardiac conditions, and so forth.

The doctrine of signatures dates back to at least the first century, and probably earlier. The physician Pedanius Dioscorides gave some credence to the doctrine, as did Claudius Galen a century later. But the doctrine of signatures had one (literally) fatal flaw. Many plant species are highly toxic when ingested, regardless of the shape and color of their leaves, blossoms, or roots. Physicians who adhered to the doctrine of signatures very often poisoned their own patients!

The problem with the doctrine of signatures is that it confuses physiology with thaumatology. Anyone with a background in magic will notice that the doctrine is nothing more or less than a variant of magic's fundamental law of sympathy. I do not think it unreasonable to suggest that the doctrine of signatures may have been extrapolated from this basic postulate of magic. The law of sympathy states that any two things resembling one another have an innate connection. This is the working principle behind the "voodoo doll". When we look at the doctrine of signatures as a variant of the law of sympathy, it can be a useful tool for herb magic. The crucial thing to keep in mind is that many plants are poisonous. No plant should ever be ingested unless you are one hundred percent certain that it is edible and non-toxic.

With this in mind, we can use the doctrine of signatures for almost any magical work, and the plants need not be limited to species associated with herbal teas and tinctures. The blossoms of the Anthurium carry a strong signature to promote sexuality. The ripened pods of Annual Honesty (*Lunaria annua*) have a signature conducive to prosperity magic, resembling silver coins. In his book *Real Magic*, Isaac Bonewits associated the six primary and secondary colors with separate magical functions; these can be considered the signatures for flower petals. Of course the doctrine of signatures can also be used for magical healing – yellow flowers for urinary problems, heart shaped leaves for circulatory problems – so long as the herbs are burned or buried or cast to the four winds, but never ingested!

The use of the doctrine of signatures is always a subjective process. We see it enacted in the movie *Practical Magic*, when young Sally Owens walks through her aunts' greenhouse gathering herbs for her "amas veritas" spell. "He will hear my call a mile away, he will whistle my favorite song, he can ride a pony backwards," she says, while picking leaves and flowers that bear the signatures for these odd requirements. "He can flip pancakes in the air, he will be marvelously kind, and his favorite shape will be a star. And he'll have one green eye, and one blue." None of Sally's herbs appear to be chosen because of their medicinal (biochemical) qualities or because of the folklore associated with them. Sally takes an entirely intuitive approach to selecting her herbs.

One simple way to use the doctrine of signatures is to brew an herbal potion at the appropriate time of the month. If you want to bring something into your life, brew the potion when the moon is in the first or second quarter (waxing). If you want to banish something, brew the potion when the moon is in the fourth quarter (waning, and less than half full). Select the blossoms and leaves that bear the signatures you want to connect with. Place these in a steeping cup, and cover them with boiling water. Now set the steeping herbs in a windowsill where they can receive the moon's rays overnight. It is not necessary to strain the herbs from the potion. The next day, after the liquid has cooled completely, take the potion outside and pour it onto the earth, saying,

"Worts, caressed by Mona's beard,
Flow now through the well of wyrd."

Mona is an early English word for 'moon', which was perceived as a masculine presence. Mona's beard, of course, refers to the moonlight. Norse Pagans may want to change the wording to Mani's beard, while Pagans whose cultures perceive the moon as feminine may prefer to change the words entirely. However, this gives a good idea of how to express your intention.

For mental fortitude or for psychic enhancement, carry a whole nutmeg seed in your pocket; it looks like a little brain. Use the red petals of a flower to arouse passion, or to improve health, since red is the color of blood. Plants with heart shaped leaves carry a signature for any kind of love spell. If you can see the resemblance between the plant and the effect you desire, the doctrine of signatures is yours to employ.

The Nine Herb Charm

By Christopher Penczak

Many of the contributions in *The Green Lovers* reference a very famous charm in Anglo Saxon lore, the Nine Herb Charm. While your typical magickal practitioner might not be familiar with it, as it comes from the *Lacnunga* text, a collection of remedies, prayers, spells and charms, the herbal magician is often quite familiar with it, and examines its herbs and appropriate use as both magick and medicine. The Lacnunga is a mix of Christian and Pagan symbolism, and often focuses upon the god Woden, known as Odin to the Norse. My introduction to it was a bit of magickal fiction based upon it, known as *The Way of Wyrd* by Brian Bates, and I highly recommend it to give you an understanding, contex,t and flavor of the material before diving deep into it if you are unfamiliar with it. Do keep in mind *The Way of Wyrd* is fiction, but a very compelling and inspiring Pagan fiction, similar, albeit less well known than *The Mists of Avalon*.

The nine herbs are somewhat a mystery, as they are mentioned by their folk names, which change over time. Many believe the nine herbs to be:

Mugwort (Mucgwyrt)
Betony (Attorlaðe)
Lamb's Cress/Water Cress (Stune)
Plantain (Wegbrade)
Chamomile (Mægðe)
Nettle (Stiðe)
Crab Apple (Wergulu)
Thyme/Chevril (Fille)
Fennel (Finule)

The nine are used in a paste to drive out poison or infections. The charm must be spoken three times over each herb as well as into the mouth, ears, and the wound of the patient. The charm is sung as each herb is added together with soap, water, ashes, and apple juice.

Nine Herb Charm

Remember, Mugwort, what you made known,
What you arranged at the Great proclamation.
You were called Una, the oldest of herbs,
you have power against three and against thirty,
you have power against poison and against contagion,
you have power against the loathsome foe roving through the land.

And you, Waybread, mother of herbs,
Open to the east, mighty inside.
over you chariots creaked, over you queens rode,
over you brides cried out, over you bulls snorted.
You withstood all of them, you dashed against them.
May you likewise withstand poison and infection
and the loathsome foe roving through the land.

Stune is the name of this herb, it grew on a stone,
it stands up against poison, it dashes against pain,
Nettle it is called, it drives out the hostile one, it casts out poison.
This is the herb that fought against the snake,
it has power against poison, it has power against infection,
it has power against the loathsome foe roving through the land.

Put to flight now, Venom-loather , the greater poisons,
though you are the lesser, you the mightier, conquer the lesser poisons,
until he is cured of both.

Remember, chamomile, what you made known,
what you accomplished at Alorford,
that never a man should lose his life from infection

after Chamomile was prepared for his food.

This is the herb that is called Wergulu.
A seal sent it across the sea-right,
a vexation to poison, a help to others.
it stands against pain, it dashes against poison,
it has power against three and against thirty,
against the hand of a fiend and against mighty devices,
against the spell of mean creatures.

There the Apple accomplished it against poison
that she the loathsome serpent would never dwell in the house.

Chervil (or thyme) and Fennel, two very mighty one.
They were created by the wise Lord,
holy in heaven as He hung;
He set and sent them to the seven worlds,
to the wretched and the fortunate, as a help to all.
These nine have power against nine poisons.
A worm came crawling, it killed nothing.
For Woden took nine glory-twigs,
he smote the adder that it flew apart into nine parts.
Now there nine herbs have power against nine evil spirits,

Against nine poisons and against nine infections:
against the red poison, against the foul poison.
Against the yellow poison, against the green poison,
against the black poison, against the blue poison,
against the brown poison, against the crimson poison.
Against worm-blister, against water-blister,
against thorn-blister, against thistle-blister,
against ice-blister, against poison-blister.
Against harmfulness of the air, against harmfulness of the ground,
against harmfulness of the sea.
If any poison comes flying from the east,
or any from the north, or any from the south,

or any from the west among the people.
Christ stood over diseases of every kind.
I alone know a running stream,
and the nine adders beware of it.
May all the weeds spring up from their roots,
the seas slip apart, all salt water,
when I blow this poison from you.

Sources

Pollington, Stephen. *Leechcraft: Early English Charms, Plantlore and Healing.* Anglo Saxon Books. Cambs, UK: 2008.

Kaldera, Raven. *http://www.northernshamanism.org/herbalism/the-nine-sacred-herbs/song.html:* March 1, 2012

http://www.odins-gift.com/pclass/nineherbs.htm: March 1, 2012

http://www.witchipedia.com/nine-herbs-charm:

http://en.wikipedia.org/wiki/Nine_Herbs_Charm

About the Contributors

Alaric Albertsson

Alaric Albertsson is the author of *Travels Through Middle Earth: The Path of a Saxon Pagan* and *Wyrdworking: The Path of a Saxon Sorcerer,* both published by Llewellyn Worldwide. His spirituality is a synthesis of Anglo-Saxon tradition, herbal studies, and rune lore. A native of the Midwest, Alaric now lives in western Pennsylvania where he continues to teach Anglo-Saxon spirituality, herbal magic, and runes. Find him online at *www.alaricalbertsson.com.*

Gwelt Awenydd

Gwelt Awenydd, A.K.A. Josiah Gromley, is an eclectic witch, freestyle shaman, Reiki master, and mystical poet living in Western Pennsylvania.

Karen Charboneau-Harrison

Karen Charboneau-Harrison is a Master of Herbology and long-time herbal alchemist. Residing in the Rocky Mountains, she is the author of the best-selling *The Herbal Alchemist's Handbook* (Red Wheel Weiser, 2011). Karen spends inordinate amounts of her time concocting magickal herbal formuals and obsessing about herbs in general.

Kenaz Filan

Kenaz Filan is the author or co-author of seven books, including *The Power of the Poppy* (Park Street Press/Inner Traditions, 2011) and, with Raven Kaldera, the forthcoming *Talking with the Spirits.* Kenaz also maintains a personal blog at *kenazfilan.blogspot.com* and a parenting blog at *witchesandpagans.com.*

Stevie Grant

Stevie Grant is a high priestess of the Temple of Witchcraft, a Reiki Master, a teacher, healer, poet, writer, and amateur musician. She and her husband Mark grow large exotic gourds at their home in the Pacific Northwest and transform them into magickally inspired gourd art.

GrayForest

GrayForest studies naturopathic medicine and magick in Seattle, Washington.

Raven Grimassi

Raven Grimassi is a published author of many titles on witchcraft and Wicca, including *Italian Witchcraft, Hereditary Witchcraft, The Cauldron of Memory,* and *Old World Witchcraft.* He is Co-Directing Elder of the Ash, Birch, and Willow Tradition, a system reflecting the commonality of European rooted traditions of Witchcraft. Raven is also Co-Director of the Fellowship of the Pentacle. He maintains a website at *www.ravengrimassi.net.*

Laura Gyre

Laura Gyre is an artist who is inspired by natural and magical themes. She lives in Pittsburgh with her husband and two children, and on the Internet at *www.ironcityalchemy.com*

Bob Hackett

Bob is an active member and priest in the Temple of Witchcraft tradition based in Salem, New Hampshire. He is currently studying High Magick (ceremonial magick) with the Temple Mystery School, but his personal practice is based on natural or shamanic magick and especially focuses on connecting with the Genius Loci, or spirits of the land, and the Tree Teachers. He also specializes in making custom made ritual tools in metal, stone, bone, and wood and can be reached through the Ancient Star Herbals page he and his wife, Irma, maintain on Facebook.

Nicole Hansche (cover artist)

Nicole Hansche, born and raised in a smallish town in southern NH would grow up to become an artist, rock climber, and fitness specialist. Though she didn't go to school for art, she has nurtured the ember, teaching herself the skills to create full blown conflagrations of color and emotion on canvas. Find her work online at *www.nicolehansche.deviantart.com* or "The Art of Nicole Hansche" on Facebook. She specializes in watercolor, acrylic and pen; sells original paintings, prints, and stickers; and is now taking commissions! Contact: *naturaspiritus@yahoo.com*

Leslie Hugo

Leslie and her husband have been growing orchids for about 10 years. They currently have over 150 orchids in their home. Leslie is a Priestess in the Temple, and practices a shamanistic approach to Witchcraft. She is also active with her local CUUPs group in Utah.

Kurt Hunter

Kurt Hunter, CADC, is a Georgian Elder and NROOGD red cord living in Portland, Oregon. He was initiated into coven-based Wicca in 1990 and continues to work within former Traditions while presently studying as an honored member of the Temple of Witchcraft. Kurt works as a professional counselor and clinical supervisor and is an avid stone collector, photographer, and cat whisperer.

Raven Kaldera

Raven Kaldera is a Northern Tradition shaman, herbalist, founding member of the Neo-Pagan First Kingdom Church of Asphodel, editor-in-chief of Asphodel Press, and author of too many books to list here. They include the *Northern Tradition*

Shamanism series, the *Northern Shamanic Herbal,* and the *Giants' Tarot.* 'Tis an ill wind that blows no minds.

Peter J. Kwiatek

Peter Kwiatek has been a student of the occult for nearly three decades. He first became interested in paganism while studying Polish language, literature, and folklore at Boston College and at the Jagiellonian University in Krakow, Poland. His interest grew while he was earning degrees in linguistics and languages the University of Delhi in India, where he learned about several aspects of Hinduism, especially Kashmir Shaivism. He has studied with Christopher Penczak for several years and is an initiate in the Temple Mystery School. He has also been initiated into the Order of Bards, Ovates and Druids, and is a frequent visitor to EarthSpirit and Temple of Witchcraft festivals and rituals. In addition to magickal practice, he is an avid promoter and performer of renaissance and baroque music played on period instruments. Peter currently lives in the hinterlands of the southern New Hampshire/Vermont border where he is eagerly fostering his skills in the Craft.

Michael Lloyd

Michael Lloyd is a chemical engineer and writer living in Columbus, Ohio. He is the author of "The History of Essential Oils" chapter of Lady Rhea's *Enchanted Formulary* (Citadel, 2007), and *Bull of Heaven: The Mythic Life of Eddie Buczynski and the Rise of the New York Pagan* (Apshodel Press, 2012). He is the co-founder and co-facilitator of the Between the Worlds Men's Gathering, an annual spiritual retreat for men who love men.

Melanie Marquis

Melanie Marquis is a lifelong practitioner of magick and the founder of United Witches global coven. She's written for national and international Pagan publications including *Circle* and *Pentacle,* and she is the author of *The Witch's Bag of Tricks*

(June 2011, Llewellyn Publications). Visit her online at *www.melaniemarquis.com* or at *www.unitedwitches.org*

Darryl McGlynn

Darryl McGlynn has been a student of the occult since the early 90's. He resides in Schomberg, Ontario, Canada where he owns thoroughbred racehorses. He has received the Munay Ki initiations as well as been trained in the Dasira Narada Immortality Study through the Human and Universal Energy Research Institute. He is also an ordained minister through the ULC Seminary. Since 2010 he has been an honored member of the Temple of Witchcraft.

Shea Morgan

Shea Morgan is an Honored Member in the Temple of Witchcraft Mystery School, serving as online moderator and mentor for the school. She is a co-founding member of her coven and a priestess of the Morrighan. Shea is a contributor to *The Temple Bell* newsletter and has contributed to Temple anthology projects, including *The Green Lovers* and the forthcoming *Waters and Fires of Avalon*. She has presented at the annual St. Louis Pagan Picnic. She lives in St. Louis, MO, with her two cats, and enjoys gardening, antiquing, spending time with coven, friends, and family, and visiting the family "century" farm; when she is not busy with her 20+ year career in government/public affairs.

Christine Moulton

My name is Christine Moulton I live in Alton, NH, and have been involved in the study of Witchcraft for about eight years. I have been mostly solitary as there are not many Witches in my area. I studied briefly under Christopher Penczak in 2000, and took the Herbal Apprenticeship in 2011 at Misty Meadows, Lee, NH.

Ann Moura

Born in 1947 and raised in a family oral tradition of Green Witchcraft learned from her mother and maternal grandmother, Ann Moura felt a need to write her heritage to pass it on and preserve it. Her adult children were raised in the Craft and, together with her daughter, she now she runs her own store, Luna Sol Esoterica, in Sanford, FL, where they present open circle public rituals for all of the Sabbats.

Ann enjoys painting, creating magical arts and crafts, and making gemstone jewelry which she sells at Luna Sol Esoterica. Her books with Llewellyn Publications include: *Green Witchcraft: Folk Magic, Fairy Lore, & Herb Craft, Green Witchcraft II: Balancing Light & Shadow, Green Witchcraft III: The Manual, Green Magic: The Sacred Connection to Nature, Grimoire for the Green Witch: A Complete Book of Shadows, Tarot for the Green Witch,* and *Mansions of the Moon for the Green Witch.* With 7th House Publishing (who publish "The Seasons of the Witch" calendars) she has Ann Moura's *New History of Witchcraft.*

Ann holds both Bachelor of Arts and Master of Arts degrees in History and writes from the perspective of her own family training and personal experience. She may be contacted by email through her websites: *www.lunasolesoterica.com* and *www.annmourasgarden.com.*

Christopher Penczak

Christopher Penczak is an award winning author, teacher and healing practitioner. His many books include *Magick of Reiki, The Mystic Foundation, The Three Rays of Witchcraft,* and *The Inner Temple of Witchcraft.* He is the co-founder of the Temple of Witchcraft tradition, a non-profit religious organization to advance the spiritual traditions of Witchcraft, as well as the co-founder of Copper Cauldron Publishing. More information can be found at *www.christopherpenczak.com.*

About the Authors

Angela Pote

I'm Angela Pote. A proud witchy mom of eight and I live in Pensylvania, I have practiced the craft for seven years, I am a priestess who follows a diverse path with a strong passion towards The Old Goddess and Gods of Ireland.

Carmen Reyes

Carmen Reyes is a dendromancer, herbalist, and educator. An ordained priestess in The Apple Branch Tradition, she serves her local and online community by teaching divination and working with moon phases.

David Salisbury

David Salisbury is a Washington, DC, based Witch practicing in the Firefly Tradition of Wicca, focusing on service and community organizing as a spiritual value. He also runs the DC bureau of the Pagan Newswire Collective.

Ruby Sara

Poet, essayist and performance artist, Ruby Sara is the author of the blog, Pagan Godspell, a member of the performance collective Terra Mysterium, and former editor-in-chief for *The Temple Bell,* official newsletter of the Temple of Witchcraft. She lives in Chicago with her intrepid spouse and their demon-monkey-cat, Pinky.

Adam Sartwell

Adam Sartwell began having psychic experiences and studying Witchcraft in his teens. He is a Reiki Master, co-founder, and Virgo lead minister of the Temple of Witchcraft, where he puts his healing and crafting skills to work making incense, candles, potions, and herbal preparations for sale to the community to raise money for the Temple.

Silvermoone

SilverMoone is a Shamanic Buddhist Witch, Clinical Hypnotherapist, priestess, teacher, healer, writer, and seeker. Her spiritual journey has taken her to the deepest layers of Self, where she finds the heart of her personal practice is devotion. Her vocation has led her to embracing the teachings of Womyn's Empowerment and Mysteries and facilitating the journey of re-birthing into Spirit.

Christine Tolf

Christine Tolf is an herbalist, flower essence practitioner and founder of Lichenwood Herbals in Barrington, New Hampshire. Christine grew up in the days when children spent all waking hours outside, free to roam the fields, forests and orchards. Today she is still most happy outside in the garden, or seeking out the wildflowers or medicinal herbs in field and woodland. She has co-created more than 200 flower essences and teaches both a three season Herbal Mentorship and a Flower Essence Practitioner Training Program while maintaining an active healing practice. For more information visit *www.lichenwood.com*.

Matthew Venus

Matthew Venus is an Artist, Rootworker, and Witch. He has been a student and teacher of the magical arts for over twenty years and is the owner and proprietor of Spiritus Arcanum (*spiritusarcanum.com*), an online occult store specializing in unique and inspirited handcrafted magical tools, artwork, jewelry, and supplies. His writing may also be found in *Hoodoo & Conjure Quarterly* and *Modern Witch Magazine,* where he is a regular contributor.

Virginia Villarred

Virginia Villarreal is from Houston Texas and is very active in the Pagan Community in the Texas area and currently the Local Coordinator and Vendor Coordinator of the Houston Pagan Pride Day, Coordinator of the GLBT Pagan Pride Float for the Houston Gay Pride Parade, Vendor Coordinator for Counsel of Magickal Arts, Coordinator of CROW (Counsel of Revolting Outrageous Women), and an honored member of the Temple of Witchcraft. She lives with her wife of eight years and together they have six children and four grandchildren.

The Temple of Witchcraft
MYSTERY SCHOOL AND SEMINARY

Witchcraft is a tradition of experience, and the best way to experience the path of the Witch is to actively train in its magickal and spiritual lessons. The Temple of Witchcraft provides a complete system of training and tradition, with four degrees found in the Mystery School for personal and magickal development and a fifth degree in the Seminary for the training of High Priestesses and High Priests interested in serving the gods, spirits, and community as ministers. Teachings are divided by degree into the Oracular, Fertility, Ecstatic, Gnostic, and Resurrection Mysteries. Training emphasizes the ability to look within, awaken your own gifts and abilities, and perform both lesser and greater magicks for your own evolution and the betterment of the world around you. The Temple of Witchcraft offers both in-person and online courses with direct teaching and mentorship. Classes use the *Temple of Witchcraft* series of books and CD Companions as primary texts, supplemented monthly with information from the Temple's Book of Shadows, MP3 recordings of lectures and meditations from our founders, social support through group discussion with classmates, and direct individual feedback from a mentor.

For more information and current schedules, please visit: *www.templeofwitchcraft.org.*

CPSIA information can be obtained
at www.ICGtesting.com
Printed in the USA
FFOW03n0459240417
34822FF